Mallard Ducks as Pets

The Mallard Duck Owner's Manual

Mallard Duck pros and cons, care, housing, diet and health all included.

by

Roland Ruthersdale

Table of Contents

Table of Contents

Foreword

While the love of animals is nearly universal, the different personalities of people affect their approach and attitudes towards pets. Essentially, different people seek different things from pets.

Some people want a furry companion with whom they can cuddle; often, such people find themselves drawn to dogs and cats. Others do not even have the desire to touch their pets and gravitate towards the aquarium hobby.

Some people prefer their pets as domesticated as possible - housetrained, hypoallergenic and tame. Others are fond of animals that not only qualify as wild animals, but also require unusual foods and intensive husbandry to maintain.

Mallard ducks are not capable of becoming house trained, and they often create a bit of a mess, but they are clearly domestic animals, having lived alongside humans for hundreds of years, if not more. However, these robust birds are self-sufficient enough to spread their wings and fly away, if their owner has not clipped their wings.

Once free of the reins of domestication, Mallard ducks carry on virtually as before, though food may be slightly harder to come by.

The most dedicated Mallard fans are often keen to learn about, observe and share their cycle of life. Even if no drake is with them, mature female Mallard ducks will deposit eggs. While they will not hatch, they provide educational lessons for youngsters, and delicious eggs for the family.

Ducks can thrive amid relatively simple accommodations, but they are also suitable for free-range keeping in a semi-natural habitat.

Mallard ducks are an important food source around the world. Many of the care information pertaining to Mallard ducks comes from duck farms interested in producing ducks for meat and eggs. It is important to understand that commercial venues do not have the same goals as pet keepers.

While the prime directive of such operations is to maximize profits, the primary goal for pet keepers is to maximize the health and happiness of their companions. Accordingly, some of the recommendations to follow may exceed the minimum necessary requirements to keep a Mallard duck alive and fit for consumption. Instead, most of the recommendations to follow will seek to find a balance between the ducks' well-being and the demands on their keepers.

Mallard ducks can make very rewarding pets, but it is important to avoid acquiring one on an impulse. Mallard duck care is not particularly difficult, but it does require significant commitment. Too many people purchase hatchling ducks at fairs or flea markets, only to realize a few weeks later that they are not comfortable providing the care the ducks need.

Contrary to what many in this situation expect, it is not easy to find a new home for your pets. Ultimately, many make the poor (and sometimes illegal) decision to release their ducks to a local pond. This is a terrible practice that must be avoided at all costs.

Mallard ducks are large, imposing waterfowl that colonize new land well. In fragile areas, these domesticated ducks may outcompete or displace native species. This can have ramifications throughout the ecosystem.

Additionally, Mallard ducks that imprinted on humans are unlikely to display the appropriate amount of fear around humans. They may be prone to aggressively begging for food, and ultimately unable to feed themselves adequately. Such ducks are also more likely to be hit by cars, take up residence in inappropriate areas and foul the landscaped and manicured properties in the area.

Accordingly, it is very important to make the decision to add Mallard ducks to your family deliberately, after careful thought and planning. Understand the husbandry requirements of the animals, and the costs you will incur.

When you bring home a duck, it is important to also understand the behavior of the bird. This is especially important if your bird will interact with other pets and animals on your farm. When you have a duck as a pet or even as a business plan, knowing how the duck will react to various situations is an absolute must. If you fail to do so, you will find yourself in many situations that you might not even be prepared for. For instance, if you are not aware of 'imprinting' as a natural phenomenon among ducks, you will be puzzled to find the hatchlings following you all around your home. When you are looking at bringing home any unique bird or animal, just knowing about providing proper care is not good enough. You must also know how to deal with various behavioral changes that may occur over time.

Taking care of the eggs and the hatchlings is just as important as taking care of the adults. If you are not equipped to do this, you will find yourself in a mess of broken and damaged eggs. Of course, the last thing you want is hatchlings that are unable to survive in your care. The care that these delicate creatures require is very different from the adults and you, as the owner, must have all the necessary information and knowledge.

Because so many ducks are bought at Easter (and most of these are impulse purchases), many caring and thoughtful breeders refrain from selling hatchlings at this time.

Despite the challenges they present, Mallard ducks make fine pets for those dedicated to their care.

This book covers all the necessary tips and information that you may require if you are bringing home a duck, for either companionship or for your business plans to be successful. This is the complete owner's manual for anyone who finds the Mallard Duck to be a fascinating option for a pet.

Chapter 1: Mallard Ducks, The Basics

1. Size and Physical Description

Mallard ducks (*Anas platyrhynchos*) are a type of breed that belongs to the category of dabbling ducks. These ducks are also part of the waterfowl family anatidae.

A Mallard Duck is a medium sized bird that is considered to be slightly larger than regular dabbling ducks. Usually, a Mallard Duck will reach an average length of about 50 to 65 cms. The wingspan of a Malard Duck is about 81 to 98 cms. The Mallard Duck, which is counted among the heaviest of all the dabbling ducks, is usually about 0.72 to 1.6 kilos or about 1/6 to 3.5 lbs in weight.

There are some standard measurements that you need to keep in mind to check if your duck is of a good quality or not. The wing chord should be between 25.7 to 30.6 cms in length, the bill should measure at least 4.4 cms and the tarsus is between 4.1 and 4.8 cms.

A male Mallard Duck that is breeding is very easy to identify. He will have a very glossy bottle green head and will have a distinct white collar that distinguishes his body from his head. The chest has a beautiful purple tinge. The wings are usually grey brown while the belly is pale grey in color. The dark tail is characteristic of a Mallard Duck. His rear is usually black in color.

A very important indication of a healthy Mallard Duck is his bill. In the case of a male Mallard, the bill is a light orange color with a visible black tip. In the case of a female Mallard, the bill is black or a speckled orange.

A mottled plumage is very typical in a female Mallard duck. The feathers show an obvious contrast between each other. Like all other dabbling ducks, female Mallard Ducks are also brown or buff in color. The eyebrows, throat and the neck are buff in color while the eye stripe and the crown are darker in color.

The one similarity between the males and the females is that they have a speculum patch. In the inner remiges, you will notice a patch of blue feathers that are purple-blue in color. These iridescent feathers make the Mallard Duck extremely attractive to look at. These feathers become very prominent when the birds are in flight. Only during the summer molting, these plumes are shed completely.

When they just hatch, the color of these birds is a bright yellow on the underside. The body is black with some traces of yellow on the face. Even the legs and the bill are black in color. When a duckling is about one month old, you will notice that the plumes have become rather drab looking. The plumes become extremely streaked. The grey coloring on the legs is also lost during this period. After two months, the duckling becomes a juvenile. When the birds are between three and four months old, the ducks are ready for to fly as their wings are fully developed at that time. It is only after this period that you will be able to distinguish between a male and a female. There are three ways in which you can distinguish between the two genders:

- The bill is black and orange in females while it is yellow in males.
- In the males, the breast feathers are reddish brown in color while in females it is brown.
- The tail feather in the centre is curled in the case of the males. In females, this feather is straight.

As the birds enter their adulthood, they become distinct in their color. This is when the males will develop the characteristic plumage colors while the females remain almost the same. You will notice a change in the plumage when these birds transition between the breeding periods. This is usually at the onset and after the molting period. A Mallard duck is considered a fully-grown adult when he is about 14 months old. The normal life expectancy for a Mallard Duck is about 3 years.

The only issue with Mallard Ducks is that they are easily mistaken to be other species. Usually it is the brown female Mallards that are considered to be other species like the Gadwall. Now, a female Gadwall has a similar orange bill with a while belly. These birds also have the typical plumage patterns as you can see on a Mallard Duck. However, if you are familiar with different breeds of ducks you will notice that the color of the plumes, although similar, will appear in various shades. For instance, the color of the plumes on the Mallard Duck is much lighter than the American black duck. Another example is the mottled duck, whose plumes do not have a white edge on the speculum.

When in captivity, Mallard Ducks can be bred to come in several colours, including white. These color variants may also be found in the domestic birds. Although the color variations in Mallard ducks are rare, the numbers are increasing due to continuous efforts by breeders.

The Mallard duck is known for their typical call. They are very noisy. The reason these ducks need special permission to keep in your backyard is that they are extremely loud. They have a very high-pitched nasal call. In females, the quack is very deep and is similar to the stereotyped duck call.

Mallard Ducks are a great example of both the Allen's rule and the Bergman's rule. These bird rules talk about the characteristics of the birds as per their geographic location. According to Bergman's rule, in comparison to their cousins in the warmer regions, the polar birds are usually larger. As per Allen's rule, the polar birds have smaller appendages to reduce heat loss. In the case of the tropical birds, these appendages are larger in order to allow heat diffusion.

2. Natural Range

It is believed that Mallard ducks are the predecessors of almost all the domesticated duck species in the word, except the Muscovies. The most important reason for the survival of this species is its ability to adapt to various habitats, food varieties and also climatic conditions. These ducks are so abundant and widely distributed that the populations of Mallards in a specific region are indicators of the overall waterfowl health in that region.

Mallard Ducks are widely distributed in both the Northern and Southern hemispheres.

In America, these birds are widely distributed in the regions between Mexico and Central Alaska. They are also found in the Hawaiian Islands.

Mallard Ducks are distributed across Eurasia, where they cover the entire area between Southern Greenland and Iceland. They are also found in North Africa, mostly in parts of Morocco. In the North, these birds are found mostly in Scandinavia. In the East, they are usually found in China and Japan.

Mallard Ducks are also found in regions of New Zealand and Australia in the Southern Hemisphere. Food abundance, habitat and human interference are the most important factors in determining the population of Mallard ducks.

3. Habitat

Mallard Ducks are believed to be the most adaptable of all the duck species. These birds not only inhabit several countries in the Northern and Southern Hemispheres, but also inhabit several climatically diverse regions. Whether it is the cold Arctic Tundra or the subtropical parts of the world, Mallard Ducks are able to live in various habitats.

They are found both in salt water and the fresh water wetlands. Usually, Mallards prefer to live in the Wetlands in order to feed and forage. They are also found in parks, lakes, estuaries, rivers and small water inlets. Sometimes the Mallard Ducks are also found in the open sea, close to the coastline. Usually, Mallard Ducks choose waters with a depth of less than 1 meter. They avoid areas that are too deep. If there is aquatic vegetation near a water body, it is likely that you will find a larger population of Mallard Ducks there.

The population of Mallard Ducks is so important that, most often, the regulations for hunting are established after the study of the distribution of Mallard Ducks in a particular region. It is ironic that although the Mallard Duck is the most hunted duck in North America, it is the population of these ducks that determines the conservation status of several species of waterfowl in a particular region.

In the year 2007, the population of the Mallard Ducks was an estimated 8.5 million in North America alone. A lull in the population of the Mallard Ducks was seen in the 1980s, along with several other species of ducks. It was due to a prolonged period of drought in the Prairie Pothole region that the population of these waterfowl decreased quite dramatically. During this time, the wetlands disappeared, making the habitat of these birds scarce. It was only in the 1990s that several conservation methods were enforced to make it possible to reinforce the numbers of the waterfowl in the region.

The Mallard Duck has been a successful species primarily because of the ability of this species to adapt and survive under several conditions.

4. Behavior

Mallards belong to a group of ducks known as dabbling ducks. These ducks belong to the family of birds known as Anatidae. Unlike other duck species that usually rely on diving to get their food, dabbling ducks only feed at the surface. The most renowned species of ducks in this family are the moa nalo, which are extinct. However, it is believed that all dabbling ducks including the Mallards are related to this extinct species.

The list of birds that belong to this family has been highly debated for several years now. While some biologists argue that only dabbling ducks should be included under the Anatinae family, others say that most ducks come under this family. Mallard ducks are among the species that have been definitely categorized under this family.

Dabbling ducks have been named so because they only eat the vegetable matter that is found on the surface. They tend to graze or upend the water surface for food. These ducks dive very rarely. These ducks are usually found near estuaries and freshwater.

The body of these birds does not allow them to dive easily. Their legs are usually placed at the centre of the body. This makes it possible for them to swim comfortably and also walk well on land. However, they are unable to dive deep in order to look for food.

These ducks are also known as "puddle ducks". Since they normally feed off the surface, they prefer to stay in waters that are not too deep. The most evident difference between dabbling ducks and diving ducks is the size of their feet. Usually puddle ducks or dabbling ducks have feet that are smaller. Since they do not need to propel themselves deep into the water to forage, they do not have very large feet.

The flight patterns of the two types of birds are also distinctly different. While dabbling ducks can easily take off from the surface, diving ducks need more force to be able to fly. They may also need to run a short distance on the water surface before taking off.

What is evident is that dabbling ducks are better fliers. In fact, they are very strong fliers. Needless to say, Mallards also maintain this characteristic trait. They are migratory birds that fly really long distances in the winter months in search of food and proper nesting. These birds leave their regular nesting sites in winter months and make trips as far as Northern Mexico. They usually choose to migrate in the beginning of the fall season.

The only things that these birds need for survival are food and a good roosting site. These birds are highly adaptable. So, when the natural foods like pondweed, wild rice and smartweed are unavailable, they simply eat grains like corn. They find these alternatives in farms and also agricultural lands. So, during the migratory period, you will see that the rice fields in the Southern Hemisphere attract large populations of Mallard Ducks. They also tend to cause a lot of damage in the process of finding something to eat.

In order to rest and feed, Mallard Ducks require wetlands or water bodies. However, for nesting, they often choose the dry ground.

Mallard ducks are social birds, which typically form small groups (primarily composed of family members) during the breeding season. When breeding is not at the forefront of their minds, they tend to form larger groups, although they do not tend to form the immense flocks that some other waterfowl do. Rarely, the ducks will live singly. Feral Mallard ducks are more likely to form mixed-species flocks than wild-living Mallard Ducks are.

Male Mallard ducks engage in intimidation behaviors to defend their territories and secure breeding rights. During such displays,

16

the drakes will raise and lower their cranial crests, bob their heads, waggle their tails from side to side, clap their beaks, hiss and peck at rivals. Males also perform similar behaviors to attract the attention of females.

Mallard Ducks are the most vocal of all the duck species. They can be extremely noisy. As I discussed before, the typical call for a male Mallard Duck is usually a loud whistle. The sound emitted by a male Mallard is extremely shrill, while the sound made by a female is a typical duck quack.

5. Reproductive Cycle

Female Mallard Ducks prefer to mate with large males that bear the largest crests. Unlike most other ducks, which form monogamous pair bonds, Mallard Ducks have a promiscuous breeding system, characterized by brief interactions (Stai, 2004).

The largest and most imposing males generally breed with several females. More than one male may breed with some females. Ultimately, most males in a given area are not able to breed, and instead form small "bachelor groups."

Wild Mallard ducks breed from August to May, during the Southern Hemisphere's summer. Domestic Mallard Ducks adapt to the climate in which they live, meaning that most captives in North America and Europe breed from March to September, in the Northern Hemisphere's summer.

Most ducks only copulate in the water. However, Mallard Ducks will breed in the water or on the land. This is consistent with the generalized terrestrial trend that Mallard Ducks exhibit, relative to mallards and other ducks.

Male ducks have spiral-shaped penises. Likewise, the vagina of females is spiraled; however, the vagina and penis spiral in opposite directions. This is believed to be an adaptation that prevents the males from forcefully breeding unwilling females.

Shortly after breeding, the female Mallard Ducks begin preparing a nest. Wild Mallard Ducks typically nest in tree hollows that are between 12 and 60 feet (4 to 18 meters) off the ground. However, some females will use secluded areas on the ground, such as hollow logs or clumps of thick vegetation. Captive Mallard Ducks usually construct their nest on the ground, in a secluded area, hidden by vegetation or other objects. The females cover the bottom of the nest with soft down feathers.

The females begin depositing one egg each day, until the nest contains approximately 8 to 16 eggs. Once the final egg has been deposited, the female begins incubating the eggs – colloquially called "sitting" or "setting" on the nest.

Until this time, the eggs remain dormant; they do not begin development until the female begins keeping the eggs warm. This causes the eggs to synchronize, so that they all hatch at roughly the same time. Otherwise, the first laid egg may hatch up to two weeks before the last egg, which would cause problems for the mother, as she would have to incubate the remaining eggs, as well as brood and feed her hatched youngsters simultaneously.

While incubating the eggs, the female will leave the nest for about one hour each day. During this time, she will eat, drink, defecate and, occasionally, bathe or swim. During this time, the eggs of wild Mallard Ducks and free-range captives are at the highest risk of predation.

Approximately 35 days later – which is about one week longer than it takes most other duck species to incubate their eggs – the eggs will "pip," meaning that the ducklings will punch through the shell and prepare to emerge from the egg. To help with the process, the hatchlings bear a calcified structure on the tip of their beaks, known as an egg tooth. The egg tooth will fall off by itself in about three or four days.

The hatchlings emerge from their eggs within about 24 hours of pipping. Upon exiting the eggs, the young ducks are wet and their down lies flat against their bodies. However, the young ducks dry quickly, and within a few hours, they appear dry and fluffy. The young have open eyes and walk well at the time of hatching, and are considered to be precocial.

The young are incapable of keeping their body temperature suitably high by themselves, so the mother keeps them warm by sitting on them and covering them with her feathers. The combination of the mother's body heat and the insulating effect of the feathers and nest keeps the young ducks warm enough until they can maintain their own body heat.

The mother will take the young ducks with her on brief excursions to obtain food and water. The mother teaches the young to drink water and forage for food on such excursions.

In most cases, Mallard males do not participate in nest construction, egg incubation or the brooding of the young hatchlings.

Is it possible for Mallards to change their gender?

It is widely believed that ducks eventually change their gender. Ducks have been known to engage in forceful sexual behavior. The drakes are usually very aggressive and might seriously injure the female in case there is competition for mating. Many animal behavior specialists believe that the "gender" change is a reaction to this type of behavior. Several duck owners have also observed a change in the sexual behavior of the females.

One characteristic difference between the male and the female is the drake feather. This is the curled feather that is found only in males. Sometimes, the female will develop this tail curl and will also develop the same coloring as the male. It is also possible that the ducks will stop laying eggs when this change in gender occurs. The reason for this change is still unknown. It remains one of those unanswered miracles of nature. However, biologists and behavior specialists have associated this change with hormonal changes.

There is another explanation to this change in the females. Hens usually have two ovaries. Out of this, one is benign and one is active. The benign ovary produces large amounts of the male hormone, testosterone. This is why the features of a drake begin to appear in a female. However, if your duck does undergo these changes, it does not mean that it has actually changed its gender. There is no ability to sire offspring. It is only the secondary sexual characteristics that are evident in these ducks.

6. Diet

Mallard Ducks are opportunistic omnivores that eat an astonishingly high variety of foods. A significant portion of their diet is made up of various aquatic and terrestrial plants, while animal prey comprises the remainder.

They consume the leaves, stems, roots, fruit, seeds and flowers of these plants. Mallard Ducks graze on grasses, forbs and herbs, similarly to geese.

Additionally, animal-based food is an important component of the diet of Mallard Ducks. They are not terribly fussy, and they will consume virtually any small creature that they can catch and overpower. Insects, spiders, worms and other invertebrates are their most common prey, but occasionally, Mallard Ducks will eat small snakes, frogs, fish and other creatures.

In Asia, Mallard ducks are often reared in ponds that are farmed for fish. While the Mallard Ducks do consume some of the small fish, they do not eat enough to outweigh the benefits the ducks provide in the form of their nutrient-laden droppings.

When feeding in the water, Mallard Ducks will "up-end" themselves to collect food from the mud below. Mallard Ducks prefer to forage in relatively shallow water, between 6 and 18 inches (15 to 45 centimeters) in depth. This is especially true for young ducks, which tend to avoid deeper water as a matter of practice.

Mallard Ducks rely on different food sources in different geographical areas. This is due in large part to their opportunistic food habits. If an unusual or unique food source is available in a given area, such as waste corn from an agricultural area, the ducks will take advantage of the opportunity.

7. Ecology

Mallard ducks fill the medium-sized, semi-aquatic, omnivorous niche. Like all animals, they interact with the species that they consume, as well as those who consume them. Additionally, they are hosts for a variety of parasites, many of which cause the ducks to exhibit few outward signs of illness.

Aquatic turtles and Mallard ducks fill a similar niche, but both groups have evolved very different strategies for surviving in these habitats. Because they are adapted in vastly different ways, the two species have enough space to occupy the same niche in these ecosystems.

While turtles live long lives, take decades to mature and produce thousands of young over their lives, Mallard Ducks rarely live a full decade, mature in their first year and – while prolific by bird standards – cannot compete with the lifelong reproductive effort exhibited by turtles.

This commonality is readily apparent when one considers that most places that hold Mallard ducks – whether naturally occurring or feral flocks - also hold turtles.

Mallard ducks likely play an important role in seed dispersal. After eating the seeds from various plants, they spread them via their droppings in the surrounding water and land areas. Some float with the current and gain a foothold on the banks downstream, sprouting and perpetuating the plant's lifecycle. Other seeds may be deposited on the land over which the ducks fly. Others may end up at the bases of the trees that the Mallard Ducks use for roosts.

In addition to helping disperse the seeds of various plants, Mallard ducks probably play an important role in preventing the uncontrolled spread of other plants. Were it not for the ducks' constant clipping of grasses and weeds, the weeds may compete with other native plants.

Similarly, Mallard ducks are important predators of a variety of insects, which helps to keep their numbers in check. Dozens of anecdotal accounts back this assertion, and many farmers and landowners rely on the ducks' appetite for insect pests to keep the pest population low. Upon dissection, many Mallard ducks are found to have esophagus's that are literally full of flying insects, such as flies and mosquitoes.

Although there are few direct observations of wild predators catching Mallard Ducks, it is likely that the ducks are important food sources for terrestrial, aquatic and flying predators.

Domestic and feral dogs, as well as their cousins, the coyotes and foxes, are some of the most important predators of the large birds. These predators do hunt the adults, but they consume many eggs and ducklings as well.

Birds of prey, including eagles, falcons and hawks capture many Mallard Ducks, especially young animals. Even large corvids, such as crows and magpies, may consume small Mallard Ducks.

In the water, adult Mallard Ducks must be wary of crocodilians and otters, while the young may also fall victim to large snakes, turtles and fish.

While humans undoubtedly consume more domestic Mallard Ducks than wild ones, humans are also predators of the ducks. Hunting pressure is one of the primary reasons that wild Mallard populations are declining along the east coast of Mexico.

8. Discovery and History with Humans

There is no exact record to state when the Mallard Duck was discovered by human beings. However, it is a fact that it is one of the oldest of all the domesticated ducks. It is also believed that most of the domestic ducks that we know of today are descendants of the Mallard Duck.

Mallard Ducks are known for their colorful plumage and have, therefore been extremely important as a decorative duck throughout human history.

In an early manuscript of the Sherbone Missal Manuscript, the Mallard Duck was an important part of the artwork. The marginal decoration of this manuscript contained beautiful illustrations of the colorful Mallard Duck. The one thing that becomes evident here is that the Mallard Duck was being domesticated and was a valuable possession even as early as the 15th Century.

The Mallard Duck, as we know already, is the most abundant species of duck found in North America. Needless to say, it is also an integral part of human civilization. There are several traditions in the modern world that include the Mallard Duck as a major part.

For instance, in the Peabody Hotel in Tennessee, the *Peabody Ducks* are extremely popular. This is a flock of four Mallard hens and one Mallard drake that have been kept in this hotel since 1933. These ducks are given the status of guests of honor in this hotel. A local farmer provides them to the hotel. Whenever a new flock is required, the old one is sent back to the farm. This rotation takes place every three months.

The Mallard Duck is also part of popular children's stories. The illustrated book "Make way for the Ducklings" was a very popular book that revolved around two Mallard Ducks who wanted to raise a family of their own.

You may also be familiar with a popular clothing brand, Duck Head, which uses a Mallard Duck Head as its logo. So, you see, from culture to trade, the Mallard Duck has made a rather important mark. It is a part of human civilization and will be for several more centuries to come.

9. Etymology

Amongst the several other bird species described by Carl Linnaeus in the book, Systema Naturae, the Mallard Duck is also included. This work, which was completed in the 18th century, lists the original biological name of the duck.

The name "Mallard" is derived from the French word *mallart or malart,* which means wild drake. Nobody knows where the origin of this French word is from. Some say that the word comes from a German male name Madelhart. There are also some alternate English words like "mawdelard" and " maudelard" from which it is believed that the names have originated.

10. Taxonomy

Taxonomy is the branch of science dedicated to classifying organisms based on their evolutionary relationships. Taxonomy helps scientists (and duck keepers) to understand the relationships of the various duck species, as well as their place in the entire tree of life.

Scientists do not always agree on exactly where some species should be placed in the tree, or which species are the most closely related. In fact, some scientists cannot even decide which animals belong to a given species and which animals do not. Accordingly, the classification of animals often changes over time, as scientists incorporate more and better data into their analyses.

Mallard ducks are members of the family Anatidae, along with geese, swans and all other living duck species. While the familial status of Mallard ducks is well established, taxonomists differ regarding more specific classification.

Historically, Mallard Ducks were considered allies of the perching ducks (subfamily Cairininae); however, this subfamily is paraphyletic, and has undergone considerable revision.

Currently, Mallard ducks are placed with the dabbling ducks, in the subfamily Anatinae. Some workers consider domestic (and by extension, feral) Mallard Ducks to be a different subspecies than their wild counterparts.

With the Mallard Ducks, there are several sub species as these birds interbreed with other ducks that belong to the same genus *anas.* This means that that the Mallard Duck will mate with birds like the American Black Duck to create several sub species. Sometimes, even distant relatives like the Northern Pintail Duck are chosen as suitable mating partners. The result of this is that there are several sub species with completely fertile adults.

This is a trait that is unique to the Mallard Duck. This is perhaps due to the rapid evolution of this species since the Late Pleistocene era. The species that have originated through interbreeding have been kept separate throughout, as their ranges are not similar. These birds may not be genetically compatible, although they have a similar lineage.

It is believed that Mallard Ducks are related closely to the Indo Pacific species rather than the American species. This is true despite the fact that these birds are more abundant in America. The biogeography of this species indicates that it is not related to its American ancestors as expected.

25

The DNA sequences of the Mallard Duck suggest that these ducks have evolved in Siberia. There have also been traces of Mallard Duck bones in the food remains and fossils that have been found across Europe. Additionally, there have been no evidences for other species that might have existed before Mallard Ducks. During the Pleistocene era, a large sub species of the ice age was also found all across Europe and West Asia. This species was named as *Anas platyrhynchos palaeoboschas.*

The Mallards in North America and the Mallards in Eurasia have been differentiated significantly. There is no genetic structure in the nuclear genome, however. When compared, the American Mallards bear genetic resemblance to mallards around the Bering Sea.

Depending upon the area that they are from, Mallards vary in size. The birds that are located in the northern hemisphere are larger and stockier and have smaller bills than the birds in the south.

The most popular variety of the Mallard Duck is the one that is found in Mexico. This duck, also called the " Mexican Duck", is found in New Mexico, Arizona, Texas and Mexico. These ducks are darker in color. They tend to interbreed with the regular Mallards that are found in the Northern parts of America. This subspecies is also known as *Anas Platyrhynchos diazi.*

11. Adaptations Made by the Mallard Duck

It is no miracle that the Mallard Duck species has survived for so many centuries. In order to make it through several generations, the Mallard Duck has made physical and behavioral adaptations according to the changing circumstances.

The Plumes

The distinct colors and the patterns on the body of the Mallard Duck are extremely important in helping the species survive. The typical coloration acts as a camouflage to protect the birds from the most common predators.

The female Mallard Ducks, especially, have a very unique color and pattern that keeps it hidden in the wild. The bird resembles reed covered wetlands and marshes. Even the young, which are the most vulnerable, have a similar pattern. On the other hand, the males have colorful plumes during the breeding season. However, in this season, their flight is powerful and they are able to protect themselves.

When the male ducks reach the eclipse molting phase, they lose the flight feathers. So, in order to stay protected in the waters until the flight feathers grow back, they also acquire the brown and mottled pattern like the females. When ducks are extremely normal looking, they tend to keep predators at bay, as they do not attract too much attention.

Caring for the Young

In the case of ducks, it is the females that do all the caring for the ducklings. Males tend to leave the females after the eggs have hatched and move on to their own flocks. The female has developed several interesting methods of protecting her young.

To begin with, when she sees a threat approaching, she will quack loudly to waylay the predator. If the predator closes in, the mother duck usually leaves the nest and keeps the ducklings behind. While this might seem cruel, it is important to know that the ducklings have been trained for a situation like this. They will remain absolutely still. As the predator lingers around, the mother duck will jump into the open water and flap around like she is injured. This takes the attention of the predator away from the little ones.

Mother Ducks are extremely brave. They will not hesitate to attack a predator when the time comes. Usually, the most common threats to the safety of the ducklings are other ducks present in the wetlands. These ducks are easily warded off by the mother duck, who will strike if she thinks that her ducklings are under attack or if the other ducks are uncomfortably close.

Flight

Mallard Ducks also have a great flying ability. These ducks just burst out of the waters and fly vertically. The Mallard Duck does not take too much time to ascend when it leaves the water. The wings are able to create an enormous force that is combined with the paddling of the feet to generate this strong propulsion.

There are several other physiological adaptations that are common to all duck species. To begin with, the webbed feet help ducks paddle in the water quickly, although the gait on land is rather awkward. In Mallard Ducks, the unique placement of the feet towards the tail helps them move better on land.

Mallard Ducks also have a flattened bill that helps them dabble well. The debris is filtered out when the duck reaches for food and gulps it down. The gizzard of the Mallard Duck is also very strong, allowing it to digest all the food that it consumes easily. Even if the duck swallows small pebbles by mistake, the stomach will be able to grind it and actually use it as roughage in the digestion process. Thus, the Mallard has survived over the years.

Chapter 2: Summary of Mallard Duck Traits

Length: 19 to 25 inches or 50 to 65 cms

Wingspan: 32 to 37 inches or 82 to 95 cms

Weight: 35 to 45 pounds or 1 to 1.3 kilos

Diet: Omnivorous. Feeds on seeds, tubers, aquatic plants and crops

Range: Usually found near wetlands.

Classification: Class: Aves

Order: Anseriformes

Sexual Maturity: 5 to 9 months

Mating Season: Spring

No of Eggs per day: 8 to 9

Other Names: Canard Colvert in French

Pato de collar in Spanish

These are some of the basic standards that you need to know to check if your bird is healthy or not. The actual breed standards required for showing and exhibiting birds are entirely different. You can check with friends who have already participated in shows to understand what breed standards are expected of a show duck. Of course, there are several manuals that have been published by special Mallard Duck clubs that you can look for online. These journals will give you a list of all the updated breed standards for the Mallard Duck.

Chapter 3: Hybrids in Ducks

It is possible to create Mallard Ducks in several color variations. While some prefer the natural look of wild Mallard Ducks, others appreciate those that have been selectively bred to bring out unusual colors and look nothing like their wild counterparts.

From a husbandry standpoint, it does not matter which color of Mallard Ducks you prefer; their care is identical. In fact, this has made it easier for breeders to combine the different color varieties and produce new and exciting variations.

For show purposes, the American Poultry Association only recognizes the natural appearance and color of these birds. However, a variety of other color mutations have been created, providing prospective owners with a diverse selection of colors to choose from.

A great deal of contradictory information surrounds the color variations of Mallard ducks. In part, this is due to misunderstandings of the mechanisms by which mutations are passed on to offspring. Before going further, it is important to review the basics behind inheritance and genetics.

1. Generalized Genetics

Virtually every facet of a Mallard duck's growth, appearance and development is controlled by its genetic code. Molecules called deoxyribonucleic acid or DNA for short carry the genetic code. Short, discrete segments of the DNA carry the code for various features of the animal, such as its gender, color and pattern. Many different genes control the colors and patterns of Mallard ducks, and these genes behave in a variety of different ways.

Wild Mallard ducks (and domestic varieties that resemble their wild counterparts) are sometimes called "wild types." These generally have a full complement of "normal" genes, although

they exhibit individual variation based on the interaction of the genes.

Through the process of domestication, people changed the appearance of the ducks as they allowed those with positive traits to breed, and culled those that had negative traits. Over countless generations, domestic Mallard ducks diverged slightly from their wild ancestors.

These ducks largely resemble their wild relatives, but they do exhibit a few key differences, such as the loss of white patches on their wings. Additionally, these ducks grow larger than wild Mallard Ducks do. Typically, these Mallard Ducks are called "black phase."

Later, random mutations appeared in the DNA of some captive Mallard ducks. Some of these traits can be passed on to the duck's offspring, but others are not inheritable and only reflect natural, individual variation.

These heritable genes generally pass from one generation to the next in predictable patterns. Each parent provides half of the DNA necessary to create a new duck, inside each sperm or egg cell. This way, when the sex cell (also called a gamete) reaches its reciprocal cell, the two create a full complement of genetic material, called their genotype.

Accordingly, Ducks usually have two copies of each gene – one from their mother and the other from their father. If these genes are identical – for example, if a duck has two copies of the white gene – the animal is called homozygous. By contrast, animals with two different versions of the same gene are called heterozygous.

A duck's genotype influences its phenotype, by instructing the body on which pigments to make and where to distribute them.

When a duck matures and is ready to breed, it will only include one version of each gene in the sperm or egg cell. Statistically speaking, half of the time the duck will include the genes from its father when making a gamete, while it will provide the mother's version of the gene the other half of the time.

Homozygous animals, which carry two copies of the same gene, have no choice but to display the trait associated with the gene. However, heterozygous animals, which carry two different genes, may or may not display the mutated gene in the phenotype, depending on the type of mutation it is.

2. Basic Patterns of Inheritance

It is possible to predict the ratio of normal and mutated genes that will usually be present in the offspring of a given pair of adults. To do so, one must know the mutations possessed by the adults, and what the pattern of inheritance associated with those genes is.

It is important to understand that the pattern of inheritance is a statistical phenomenon. Any given clutch may violate the predictions of the model, but given enough eggs, the predictions hold true.

Dominant Genes

Dam / Sire	Normal	Heterozygous	Homozygous Mutant
Normal	All Normal	50% Normal 50% Heterozygous Mutants	All Heterozygou s Mutants
Heterozygous	50% Normal 50% Heterozygou s Mutants	25% Normal 50% Heterozygous 25% Homozygous	50% Heterozygou s Mutants 50% Homozygous
Homozygous Mutant	All Heterozygou s Mutants	50% Heterozygous Mutant 50% Homozygous Mutant	All Homozygous Mutant

Dominant genes are displayed phenotypically when present. Most of the common traits of a species are dominant, as recessive genes are eventually weeded out of wild gene pools, unless they are neutral (do not cause hardship for those displaying the trait) or offer a selective advantage.

Dominant traits are expressed whether the animal is homozygous or heterozygous. There is no difference in the appearance of the two varieties; the only difference manifests when such animals are bred.

Homozygous mutants only produce other mutants, while heterozygous mutants can produce normal and mutant offspring.

Dominant color patterns of Mallard ducks include the wild-type appearance and the white-headed (Canizie) mutation.

Incompletely Dominant Genes

Sire \ Dam	Normal	Heterozygous	Homozygous Mutant
Normal	All Normal	50% Normal 50% Heterozygous	All Heterozygous
Heterozygous	50% Normal 50% Heterozygous	25% Normal 50% Heterozygous 25% H	50% Heterozygous 50% Mutant
Homozygous Mutant	All Heterozygous	50% Heterozygous 50% Homozygous Mutant	All Homozygous Mutant

Incompletely dominant traits express themselves partially when only one copy of the gene is present. When paired with another copy of the gene, such mutations are expressed fully in the animal's phenotype.

Breeding projects involving incomplete dominance can yield animals with three different phenotypes: Normal, heterozygous animals and homozygous mutants.

The blue-dilution and white mutations are both examples of incompletely dominant traits.

Co-Dominant

Dam Sire	Normal	Heterozygous (Intermediate Phenotype)	Homozygous Mutant
Normal	All Normal	50% Normal 50% Heterozygous (Intermediate Phenotype)	All Heterozygous (Intermediate Phenotype)
Heterozygous (Intermediate Phenotype)	50% Normal 50% Heterozygous (Intermediate Phenotype)	25% Normal 50% Heterozygous (Intermediate Phenotype) 25% Mutant	50% Heterozygous (Intermediate Phenotype) 50% Mutant
Homozygous Mutant	All Heterozygous (Intermediate Phenotype)	50% Normal 50% Heterozygous (Intermediate Phenotype)	All Mutant

Co-dominant traits are very similar to incompletely dominant traits, in that the heterozygous form displays a mutated phenotype.

Co-dominant traits produce animals with intermediate phenotypes. The classic example occurs when red flowers (a co-dominant trait) are crossed with white flowers (another co-dominant trait) to produce pink flowers. Co-dominant traits work somewhat similarly to incompletely dominant traits, as usually the homozygous form of the trait produces an increased effect, relative to heterozygous individuals. These two terms are often confused and misapplied.

There are no truly co-dominant color mutations for Mallard ducks, but the term is sometimes applied to the white and black color forms, because the product of a black and white animal is a "pied" animal that displays both black and white pigment. However, the white color mutation is incompletely dominant, whereas black coloration is dominant.

Simple Recessive

Dam Sire	Normal	Heterozygous	Mutant
Normal	All Normal	50% Normal 50% Heterozygous	All Heterozygous
Heterozygous	50% Normal 50% Heterozygous	25% Normal 50% Heterozygous 25% Mutant	50% Heterozygous 50% Mutant
Mutant	All Heterozygous	50% Normal 50% Heterozygous	All Mutant

Recessive traits are only expressed in homozygous individuals, except in the case of sex-linked genes (discussed below). Heterozygous individuals carry one copy of the mutated gene and may pass it on to their offspring, even though they do not display the gene. In fact, two normal appearing, heterozygous animals can produce young which have both copies of the gene. These homozygous offspring will display the mutated trait, even though their parents looked completely normal.

Simple recessive traits are only visible in homozygous individuals. Unfortunately, there is no way to determine which animals are heterozygous visually. Breeding trials are the only way to be certain that an animal is a heterozygous individual. If an animal produces a mutant, it must be heterozygous for the trait, as such mutations must be passed on by both parents.

In some cases, an animal may be heterozygous for a recessive trait, or it may be completely normal. For example, if a Duclair piebald male mates with a normal-appearing female, all of the young will have one copy of the Duclair gene – making them heterozygous.

If one of these ducklings attains adulthood and breeds a normal partner, some of the resulting offspring will be heterozygous. The problem is, you cannot tell which ones are and which ones are not. Statistically speaking, about half of the offspring are heterozygous, while the other half are not. So, when such young are sold, they are described as being 50 percent possible heterozygous. This means that if you purchase one of these young, there is a 50 percent chance that it carries the Duclair gene.

Similarly, if two heterozygous individuals produce offspring, each individual (other than any homozygous Duclairs) has a 66% chance of being heterozygous.

Simple recessive traits are the most common type of mutation found in Mallard ducks. The barred, brown-rippled, lavender, sepia and Duclair piebald trait are all simple recessive traits.

Sex-Linked Recessive

Dam / Sire	Normal (Does Not Display Mutant Trait)	Mutant (Displays Mutant Trait)	Mutation only occurs on the "W" chromosome – there are no homozygous females.
Normal (Does Not Display Mutant Trait)	All Normal	50% Normal Females 50% Heterozygous Males (Do Not Display Mutant Trait)	
Heterozygous (Does Not Display Mutant Trait)	25% Normal Females 25 % Normal Males 25% Mutant Females 25% Heterozygous Males (Do Not Display	25% Normal Females 25% Heterozygous Males (Do Not Display Mutant Trait) 25% Mutant Females 25%	
Mutants	50% Heterozygous Males	All Mutants	

	(Do Not Display Mutant Trait) 50% Mutant Females		

Sex-linked mutations are those that occur on the sex chromosomes. Accordingly, their pattern of inheritance is different for males and females. The chocolate trait is the only sex-linked trait described for Mallard ducks.

Most gene mutations that affect the color of Mallard ducks are located on the autosomal genes. These genes are identical in both males and females, and the pattern of inheritance does not vary between the sexes. In other words, males and females are affected equally by the mutation.

Sex-linked traits work differently. Ducks have genotypically determined gender, meaning that the DNA of the parents determines the sex of the offspring. This contrasts with crocodilians and turtles, whose gender is determined by environmental conditions.

For example, in humans, those with two "X" chromosomes become female, while those that have one "X" chromosome and one "Y" chromosome become male. When adult females produce sex cells, they always receive an "X" chromosome, because that is all that the female has to contribute. By contrast, males donate an "X" chromosome about half of the time and a "Y" chromosome the other half of the time. Each sperm cell has one or the other, so male humans determine the gender of their offspring. This is called XY sex determination.

Mallard ducks (and most other birds that have been studied) exhibit a similar system, although key differences exist.

Mallard ducks exhibit ZW sex determination. Females are the heterogametic sex, while males are the homogametic sex. Males have two "W" chromosomes, while females have one "W" chromosome and one "Z" chromosome.

This means that if a mutated gene occurs on the "Z" chromosome, males cannot express the trait. However, it also means that if a trait occurs on the "W" chromosome, females must display it phenotypically, as there is no other gene to express dominance over it.

Males – who possess two "W" chromosomes – may have the mutant trait, but not express it, because it has a normal (and dominant) version of the gene to repress the expression of the mutant.

Ultimately, this means that a female cannot carry a sex-linked trait without expressing it. Males, on the other hand, may very well have the "hidden" trait.

Natural Appearance

Male Mallard ducks will have a very glossy, bottle green head and will have a distinct white collar that distinguishes his body from his head. The chest has a beautiful purple tinge. The wings are usually grey brown while the belly is pale grey in color. The dark tail is characteristic of a Mallard Duck. His rear is usually black in color.

A female Mallard Duck usually has a mottled plumage. They are usually brown in color with white feathers to contrast the major body color. This is a color pattern that is found in several other ducks that belong to this family. Therefore, there are at least seven other duck types that are difficult to distinguish from the female mallard. We will discuss about these ducks in more detail in the following chapters.

Hatchlings are predominately black, with variable amounts of yellow on the belly and face. They have a bold, dark stripe that extends posteriorly from their eye." They gradually increase the amount of dark coloration as they grow. Juvenile wild Mallard Ducks are duller than the adults are, and they have relatively fewer white feathers on the wings and body.

In captivity, it is possible to have several colors of Mallard Ducks including white. However, the wild type coloration is most preferred and is characteristic of a Mallard Duck.

The most important thing with Wild Ducks is that they are capable of interbreeding with several other species. This has given rise to several other sub species that have coloration similar to the Mallard Duck. In the following chapter, we will discuss in detail about the similarities and differences between the regional sub species that are found commonly.

Chapter 4: Ducks Similar to the Mallard Duck

The Mallard Duck is known for interbreeding with other ducks that belong to the same species. As a result, there are several sub species that have evolved over the years. These ducks are uncannily similar to the Mallard Duck and are therefore very difficult to identify. Here are seven duck species that can be easily mistaken for Mallard Ducks. The similarities and the differences mentioned here will help you identify a Mallard Duck.

American Black Duck

Resembles:

A female Mallard Duck or a Male Mallard Duck during the eclipse season.

Differences:

- The color of the plumage is darker
- A distinct black border on the blue patch seen on the wing
- Darker tail

Mottled Duck

Resembles:

A female Mallard Duck or a Male Mallard Duck during the eclipse season.

Differences:

- The face is very pale
- The throat is unmarked and buffy
- Darker tail

Gadwall

Resembles:

Adult Female Mallard Duck

Differences:

- The head is blockier in comparison to the well-rounded head of the Mallard Duck.
- The body has a silver-gray coloration that is finely patterned.
- The wings have a warm brown wisp.
- The head has a dual tone with a dark shade above and a paler shade below.
- The Female Gadwall has a two toned bill that has a black tone above and an orange tone below.
- In the females, the white patch is seen even when the wing is folded.

Northern Shoveler

Resembles:

Adult Male Mallard

Differences:
- The wing has a distinct sky blue patch.
- The chest is white with flanks that are a dark chestnut brown color.
- The bill is broad and spatulate

Red Breasted Merganser

Resembles:

Male Adult Mallard

Differences:

- The neck has a bold white collar
- The chest has a distinct shape with a shaggy crest.
- The bill is serrated.
- Distinct white stripes on the sides demarcate the gray flanks from the back.

Although it is not easy for a novice to be completely sure of the differences and similarities between the different species of ducks, it is possible to learn how to identify them with practice. However, if you are going to be a first time owner of a Mallard Duck pet, you may want to seek a reputed breeder to ensure that you do not end up with the wrong variety.

If you are interested in breeding ducks, it is a lot more important for you to ensure that you bring home the right species. If you bring home one of the similar cousins of the Mallard duck, you might find several behavioral problems, including aggression, as two sub species may not be entirely compatible.

The quality of the egg may also be compromised if you bring home different sub species. If you are unsure about distinguishing between different subspecies, there are experts who can help you out at a small cost. It is recommended that you bear these costs to ensure that your flock consists of pure Mallards that are entirely worth the investment.

Chapter 5: The Mallard Duck as a Pet

Now that you know the basics of Mallard ducks, and have been tempted by the myriad of colors and patterns that the ducks come in, you must decide if they are a good fit for you and your family.

1. Understanding the Commitment

Mallard ducks can make wonderful companions, but they are not good pets for everyone. Keeping any animal is a serious commitment, and Mallard Ducks are no exception. Be sure that you understand exactly what your responsibilities will be and that you are willing to perform them before adding a Mallard to your family.

You will have to purchase commercial food for your Mallard Ducks, and give it to them daily. Additionally, you will need to provide your ducks with regular access to a place to forage for grasses, seeds and invertebrates. You may also have to confine the ducks to a pen or roost each night and then release them in the morning. It can take quite some time to coral the ducks, although some learn to anticipate the daily activity and may do so with little encouragement from you.

Your ducks will need a safe and appropriate place to live. While some people may have ample space and the appropriate type of setting to allow their ducks to range freely, others may have to construct a pen to contain them. They will also need windbreaks and shelters to keep them from being exposed to rain or cold winds. Finally, while Mallard Ducks are not as aquatic as mallard-derived breeds are, they still desire at a small pond for swimming and bathing.

45

You will have to keep your Mallard Ducks' living area and pond clean, which can take a significant amount of effort. Mallard Ducks, like all ducks, eat a lot of food and produce an equally impressive amount of waste. While this waste is biodegradable, the process of biodegradation takes some time to occur.

If you only have a few ducks and they live in a very large area, their waste may breakdown fast enough to avoid accumulating. However, in most scenarios, you will be forced to remove this waste on a regular basis. While duck droppings are a nutritious additive for lawns and compost heaps, the sheer volume of droppings produced by the ducks may challenge your patience and commitment.

You will have to find a veterinarian that is qualified to care for your ducks, should any of them become sick. You will also have to do something with the endless eggs that the ducks deposit, and, if a drake is kept with the ducks, the large number of ducklings that will emerge from those eggs.

If one of the ducks gets sick, you will have to arrange for prompt treatment and, often, a separate living area. This will help keep the ducks from spreading diseases among themselves.

2. Geographic Concerns

Temperature

Because wild Mallard Ducks are native to the tropics, they are usually quite comfortable living in warm climates. However, it is always imperative to provide the birds with deep shade and a swimming pool during hot weather.

Mallard ducks are also quite cold hardy, and more resistant to cold temperatures than chickens are. However, they do require warm sleeping quarters during the winter if the external temperatures fall too low. Nevertheless, research has demonstrated that Mallard ducks vary the metabolic processes of their muscles and livers to offset and acclimate to cold temperatures (Fernando GogliAntonia Lanni, 1993).

If you live at northern latitudes, you may have to create structures in which the ducks can retreat from the cold. In extremely cold climates, it may be necessary to place heat lamps in the shelter. Another problem faces keepers of Mallard Ducks that live in cold climates; you must find some way of converting their water reservoir from an ice skating rink back into a pond each morning. While water reservoirs in moderate climates may only freeze at the surface, and can be easily broken or melted to provide water access for the ducks, ponds in very cold regions are likely to freeze solidly. It requires a great deal of energy to melt such ponds, so be sure you have devised a plan to deal with this situation before you add Mallard ducks to your family.

Rainfall and Humidity

Mallard ducks hail from relatively humid environments with ample rainfall, so they are likely to thrive in even the rainiest climates. In contrast, they are not specifically adapted to arid habitats, but given a large water reservoir, they are unlikely to suffer from any humidity-related problems.

Social and Legal Considerations

Mallard ducks are so hardy, adaptable and loved by humans that they have colonized a number of areas outside their natural range. In the United States, both Florida and Texas have breeding populations of the birds. Similar feral populations have been reported in Canada and Europe as well.

Many wildlife professionals consider Mallard ducks to be a potentially problematic addition to natural ecosystems. While no evidence of Mallard-caused harm has been collected yet, these large, robust and prolific waterfowl may indeed outcompete many native species.

This has led some jurisdictions to place restrictions on the keeping of Mallard ducks. Always check with your local animal control office, wildlife management department or law enforcement agency before acquiring Mallard ducks. Even if Mallard ducks are legal in your area, it is important that Mallard ducks are not allowed to escape, nor should they be purposely released, to avoid exacerbating this problem.

Even if Mallard Ducks are not able to colonize your area, they may spread disease to other species of waterfowl, before they pass away or move. This can cause potentially catastrophic results for wild ecosystems.

3. Pros and Cons

Pros	Cons
Mallard ducks are highly decorative because of their colorful plumage.	Mallard duck females and juvenile males are capable of flight, unless their wings are clipped or pinioned.
Mallard ducks live for about 8 years.	Mallard ducks are much larger than the more commonly kept, white Pekin ducks.
In contrast to Pekin ducks and other breeds derived from wild mallards, Mallard ducks do not spend as much time in the water.	Handling Mallard ducks is difficult, potentially dangerous and stressful for the birds. They are very noisy and loud. Care must be exercised when restraining or manipulating adult birds.
Migration is not a regular part of the Mallard duck lifecycle, although they will move short distances to avoid inclement weather.	Mallard ducks are prone to pecking their cage mates when overcrowded.
Many people find that their Mallard Ducks become very tame, friendly companions.	Mallard ducks may sometimes be aggressive.
Mallard ducks are prolific egg layers that will keep your family stocked in eggs.	Mallard ducks are prolific egg layers that may produce more eggs or chicks than you can easily accommodate.

4. Myths and Misinformation

Myth: *Mallard ducks are mean and aggressive.*

Fact: Male Mallard ducks are aggressive towards each other, and some drakes do react aggressively towards humans. However, most drakes become friendly, loyal companions if raised with love and attention from a young age. Most female Mallard Ducks are very gentle with people.

Part of their aggressive reputation may stem from their large size, which can be intimidating to some. Combined with the aggressive begging habits of feral ducks and their unusual appearance, it is easy to understand how this largely misguided reputation came to be.

Myth: *You can get rich breeding Mallard ducks.*

Fact: While you can certainly raise and breed Mallard ducks with relative ease, you are highly unlikely to generate a significant revenue stream from a flock of pet ducks. Even if you have three female ducks, and each lays 100 eggs in a year, you only have 300 eggs. Most large-scale commercial productions produce millions of ducks annually. To say you are at a competitive disadvantage would be an understatement.

Myth: *Ducks can live inside as dogs or cats can.*

Fact: The Center for Disease Control and Prevention strongly cautions against keeping poultry in living spaces. Among other problems, ducks can transmit Salmonella to their human keepers. Salmonella may only cause healthy adults some gastrointestinal distress, but it can be fatal for children and the elderly. Your ducks can be part of the family, but they belong outside (or in dedicated buildings).

Myth: *If you touch a Mallard Duck's caruncled skin, you will get warts.*

Fact: Utterly false. The caruncled skin is completely harmless to touch. It feels soft, dry and somewhat rubbery. However, as with any other animal, you should always wash your hands with soap and water after touching Mallard Ducks.

Myth: *Mallard ducks will always stay in your yard if you feed them well.*

Fact: While it is true that Mallard ducks tend to stay in the same area as long as their needs are met, and they do not migrate, nothing prevents them from flying away. Clipping or pinioning their wings does prevent them from flying, but is an undesirable option in the minds of some. Each keeper will have to decide if their ducks' wings will be altered or if they can live with the relatively remote possibility that the birds will fly off.

Myth: *When you breed two Mallard ducks of different colors, their offspring will exhibit a blend of their colors.*

Fact: In some cases, such as the offspring from one black parent and one white parent, the offspring will exhibit varying amounts of black and white pigment. However, the various color mutations of the species work in a variety of ways. By understanding the pattern of inheritance among the various colors, it is possible to predict the type of offspring a given pair will produce.

Myth: *If your ducks look healthy and clean, they are probably free from diseases.*

Fact: Nothing could be further from the truth. Often, ducks carry sub-clinical infestations of bacteria, viruses or protozoa. While they may not be suffering from the symptoms that are characteristic of the disease, they may still harbor the pathogen and be able to spread it.

Salmonella is an excellent example of such a disease. Most ducks probably harbor the bacteria in their bodies, yet they often exhibit no outward signs of illness. Nevertheless, these animals can spread the infection to humans and other animals. Accordingly, strict hygiene is always required when caring for ducks.

Chapter 6: Acquiring Mallard Ducks

Acquiring a Mallard duck is more complicated than simply walking in your local pet store and walking out with some new pets. You must ensure that you only purchase healthy ducks, you must be sure to purchase the right ratio of males and females, and you must decide on the best place to shop for the ducks.

1. Selecting a Healthy Pet

When selecting a pet Mallard duck, always strive to acquire the healthiest birds available.

Ill, stressed or injured animals may display any of the following signs:

- Cloudy, swollen or sunken eyes

- Smeared fecal material near their cloaca

- Wings that do not lie flat against the body of the bird, that dangle limply or exhibit any other deformity of lack of function.

- Birds that have visible sores, wounds or areas of missing feathers (do not confuse the scruffy appearance of a molting duck with that of a duck with a health problem).

By contrast, healthy animals will exhibit:

- Strong interactions with other members of the flock

- Strong legs and rapid, purposeful movement

• Healthy appetites. Ducks should eat eagerly when fed, and drink water shortly afterwards

2. Social Considerations

It is not advisable to acquire a single Mallard duck, whether male or female. Mallard ducks are very social birds that will imprint on the animals with which they interact. If they do not have another bird to socialize with, they will imprint on their keeper. While this can make the duck more comfortable in your presence and foster a strong owner-pet bond, the bird will fail to learn how to socialize with other birds.

This is primarily a problem if you decide to add other ducks at a later date. The original bird will not have the capability of existing peacefully in the new society and will be prone to fighting with its cage mates.

Another occasion in which this might cause a problem is if you are forced to place your duck in another home. If, for example, your job requires you to relocate and you are unable to care for your duck, it will be difficult to find a new home for the bird. Having imprinted on you, it will be stressed out being separated from you, and the bird will have to go to a home that does not have any other ducks.

In general, you should purchase at least three or four ducks. Ideally, you will purchase one drake and two or three females, which is an optimum ratio for most pet owners.

It can be difficult to determine the gender of Mallard ducks while they are very young. Accordingly, it makes sense to purchase slightly older ducks that are easily identifiable by gender. Alternatively, breeders and veterinarians can often distinguish between the genders by examining their cloaca (often called the duck's "vent").

3. Buying from Breeders or Hatcheries

Most Mallard ducks are purchased from breeders, and there are many reasons for this. One is that breeders are among the first results to pop up in a typical Internet search; pet stores do not often carry ducks year-round, so they do not advertise them as much.

Another reason why breeders are one of the most desirable avenues through which to acquire a Mallard duck is sheer selection. Few breeders of Mallard ducks produce only one variety; most breeders have four, five or more variations from which you can choose.

Additionally, breeders are generally better informed about the genetics of the ducks they have available. This is important if you seek to breed your ducks and produce different varieties yourself.

An underappreciated benefit of purchasing a Mallard duck from a breeder is that you can be more certain that you obtain unrelated animals. This is important to prevent inbreeding, which can cause the ducks to produce offspring with health problems.

When purchasing animals directly from a breeder, you have the ability to ensure that your animals have been treated well prior to you purchasing them. This is not the case when purchasing birds from retail establishments, as the ducks may have passed through the hands of multiple wholesalers before reaching the retail store.

Finally, the quality of stock offered by breeders is generally superior to the quality available through other avenues.

4. Buying from Retailers

While retail establishments seldom breed Mallard Ducks, they may carry hatchlings from time to time, particularly in the spring. Usually Pekin ducks are more common at pet stores, but Mallard ducks can be found at such establishments with ample effort.

The benefits of buying from a retail establishment are numerous. You will usually have your choice among many ducks, you can often hold and interact with them to ascertain their personality and you can see how the birds eat, drink and get along with their cage mates.

Additionally, and perhaps most importantly for new duck keepers, the pet store can provide care information and easy access to some of the supplies you will need. In addition, most pet stores will provide some sort of health guarantee for the ducks.

However, these things come at a price, and ducks will cost much more in a pet store than they will if purchased from a breeder. Nevertheless, typical, pet-quality Mallard ducks are modestly priced. Even if the retailer doubles the price you would pay a breeder, the total difference in price will still be relatively modest.

5. Buying from Individuals

Often, one of the best places to get Mallard ducks is from other pet keepers and duck enthusiasts. Many people acquire Mallard ducks only to become overwhelmed by the numerous chicks they end up with. These people often try to sell their surplus, but find it a challenging prospect and end up giving away most of the hatchlings.

The problem is that it can be hard to locate such people. The best way to do so is by frequenting online message boards and perusing the local classified sections.

6. The Cost of Mallard Ducks

The price you will pay for your Mallard ducks depends on whether you purchase them from a breeder, retailer or individual, as well as the number you purchase, the gender of the ducks and the color varieties selected.

In general, hatchlings that display common colors vary from about $4.00 to $30.00, (£2 to £18) depending on the quantity purchased and the place they were purchased from.

However, the prices for rare color varieties can be astronomical. In 2012, an award-winning drake sold for £1,500 at auction ($2,500) (Mail, 2012).

It is difficult to predict the setup and ongoing costs involved with keeping Mallard ducks. If you already have an enclosed area with a pond, or only plan on providing the ducks with a small children's pool, your startup costs will be fairly low. In contrast, if you plan to fence in a large area, build an elaborate pond or construct stand-alone buildings, the costs can reach into the thousands.

While it may be possible to save some money by purchasing used equipment, such as feeding dishes, watering systems and feather clippers, resist the urge to do so. Usually, the savings are minimal when the potential for disease spread is factored into the equation.

7. Adopting Mallard Ducks

The last option available to Mallard Duck lovers is adoption. This option is suitable for you if you are looking for a duck that you don't have to shell out too much for. Of course, adoption is also a very noble thing to do, as you will be able to provide a rescued duck a loving home.

There are several shelters and rescue homes where you will be able to find Mallard Ducks for adoption. When you are looking at adopting a duck, there are some things that you must keep in mind:

- Make sure you check the health of the duck thoroughly. Ducks may have several infections that are dangerous for people, especially salmonella.
- Be prepared for behavioral issues if your duck has had an abusive past.

- Make sure that you are able to afford necessary treatments if required.

When you are sure that you will be able to take the responsibility, you may adopt a loving Mallard Duck.

8. Should You Bring Home Ducks or Ducklings?

For new duck owners, this can be a very difficult question. Should you bring home an adult duck? Or should you experience the joy of actually raising a duckling till it is an adult? The answer is quite simple. It entirely depends upon what your real intention of bringing home a duck is.

For those who already have ducks at home, bringing an adult into the group is a safer bet than bringing home a duckling. A group of ducks is less likely to adopt a duckling. However, their chances of getting along with an adult bird are higher. Another reason for bringing home an adult duck is adoption. If you want to give shelter to a wounded or abandoned duck, it is a great and noble ideal. However, with these ducks you must take necessary precautions and quarantine measures.

Of course, many prefer a duckling, as they want to actually rear the little bird and experience the entire process. You can buy ducklings from animal shelters and also pet stores. If you are already into duck farming, hatching an egg is also a good option to bring home a duckling.

There are several benefits of bringing home an adult duck or a duckling. The only determining factor for you to make this choice is the reason you want to have a pet duck.

Benefits of a Duckling

- You can actually take care of the bird from scratch. From the bedding to the shelter, you can take care of all the elements needed to make the duckling feel at home.

- The temperament of the duckling will be as per your approach to bringing up. You can train them to be highly sociable and gentle when you rear them from the baby years.
- It is easier to make a duckling personable. You can teach them tricks easily when they are ducklings.
- You can be sure of the health of your duckling. Since it has been with you all along, you can be certain that it is free from parasites and infections.
- If you are looking at raising ducks in a farm alongside other animals, it is advisable to bring home ducklings. They are able to get along with other animals easily when they grow up in the same environment.

Benefits of Ducks

- If you want to your duck to be an addition to an already existing group of pet ducks, an adult duck is a better choice.
- Those who are looking at a lucrative business will benefit by including healthy adult ducks instead of ducklings. There is no need to wait for the duckling to grow into an adult. You can also save on the investments required to raise a duckling.
- You can provide a safer environment to a duck that has been abandoned or orphaned.
- Exhibitors benefit by bringing home well-bred show ducks instead of ducklings. The cost of raising is reduced in this case.

Irrespective of whether you are bringing home an adult duck or a baby duck, you must be highly cautious about the health of the bird. In several cases, even a healthy looking duck might carry salmonella in its feathers and feet. So taking ample quarantine measure is important when you are considering a pet duck.

Chapter 7: Housing Your Pet Duck

There are a variety of different strategies that keepers use to keep their Mallard ducks healthy, safe and comfortable. Each strategy has benefits and drawbacks, meaning that few choices are "right" or "wrong."

Some keepers enjoy providing their ducks with luxurious fields for foraging and expansive ponds for swimming and bathing, while others keep their ducks in concrete-floored pens with drinking water, but no water for swimming.

Some keepers place a premium on ensuring that their ducks cannot escape, nor be reached by predators; whereas others place no pens, fences or roofs over their animals, and simply hope for the best.

Keepers in sub-tropical climates may not find it necessary to provide shelter for their ducks at night, while keepers in the far north may be forced to provide heated shelters to ensure their Mallard Ducks do not fall ill.

Ultimately, the keeper will have to determine the best method for housing his or her ducks. No matter which style of housing you provide your animal, you must address a few common issues. For example:

•   The enclosure must allow the ducks adequate space to extend their wings fully and obtain enough exercise.

•   The enclosure must allow the ducks enough individual, "personal" space to ensure they remain stress free and to keep pecking and infighting to a minimum.

• The enclosure must have appropriate temperatures for the ducks. While ducks require much higher temperatures when they are young, the optimum temperature for adults is about 55 degrees Fahrenheit. Fully feathered Mallard Ducks can tolerate much lower temperatures, but they require shelter to retreat from the winds and heavy rain. The ducks must be able to retreat to the water or shade if the temperatures reach 90 degrees or more.

• The keeper must decide on the desired security level of the duck's area. Mallard ducks do not migrate, but they can fly and may decide to leave. To eliminate the possibility of escape, the duck's area must be enclosed on all sides. Clipping their wings may eliminate them from flying away, but they may still escape on foot or by water.

• Related to the issue of keeping the ducks inside the enclosure, the keeper must decide on the degree to which the enclosure is secure from predators. A roof or net is the only thing that will completely protect the ducks against hawks and owls. Complete security may not even be possible in such cases, as snakes, rats and weasels can penetrate very small holes.

• The enclosed area must be safe for the ducks. Care should be taken to ensure that no plants that are toxic to ducks are in the enclosed space. No sharp or dangerous objects should be in the cage, and the substrate should be suitable for the duck's feet.

• The enclosure must be placed in an area that is suitable for ducks. They should not be housed near food preparation areas, such as backyard barbeque pits and picnic areas. They should not be housed adjacent to areas where dogs or children roam, nor should they be housed immediately next to roads or driveways.

1. Housing for Hatchlings

When you purchase your first group of Mallard ducks, it is best to start with a group of hatchlings. Given that their mother will not be there to keep them warm and safe, you will have to provide these services for them.

Housing the Hatchlings

The best way to house your first Mallard Ducks is in an indoor pen or cage. However, the indoor area should not be in a living area. Auxiliary buildings, insulated sheds and detached garages are the best choices.

Hatchlings are among the most vulnerable ducks to predators, and without their mother to protect them they are unlikely to dissuade hungry foxes, hawks or snakes.

Keeping the ducks indoors eliminates the vast majority of predators, allows you to keep a close eye on the little ducklings and is an easy place in which to keep them warm.

The downside of indoor duck maintenance is the mess and smell that will emanate from cages that are not cleaned diligently. Accordingly, you must commit to cleaning the cage every day (perhaps twice per day if the ducks do not enjoy plenty of space). This is not only important for the air quality, but also for the little ducks' health and well being. It is important to clean both the land area and the water in the cage.

At its most basic, an indoor duck pen consists of an enclosed space, that is outfitted with a heat lamp (or two) and a water container. While it may not be strictly necessary for the water container to be large enough to permit swimming, it will greatly improve the young ducks' quality of life if you provide such opportunities. Regardless, ducks absolutely require clean drinking water throughout the day.

The walls of the enclosed space can be constructed, so that they rest on the floor, or they can be provided via a container. In other words, you may choose to connect several boards to form the walls of the enclosure, or you may choose to use a very large container to form the ducks' enclosure.

The floor of the pen should be covered in soft bedding, such as straw or clean paper (butcher's paper, newsprint, etc.). You can also use bare floors if they are not too cold, but they will require daily cleaning.

Keeping the Hatchlings Warm

It is crucial that the young hatchlings are able to stay warm. If they become chilled, they can become sick and die with alarming rapidity. In the wild, Mallard mothers brood their young as necessary during this time; but as most people start with hatchlings (and therefore no mother is present), you will have to ensure the young stay warm.

Young hatchlings have two things working against them that make it hard for them to keep warm. Most obviously, the young birds do not yet have the full suite of feathers that the adults have. These feathers are very effective at insulating the adults, and without them, the young are susceptible to hypothermia.

Secondly, but just as importantly, hatchling ducklings are very small, compared to the adults. This means that the ducklings have a very high amount of surface area, relative to their internal volume, when compared against the surface to volume ratio of adults.

When all other things are equal, the higher the surface to volume ratio of an animal is, the more rapidly it will radiate heat. This means that little ducklings radiate a greater percentage of their internally produced heat per unit of time than the larger adults do. Fortunately, as they grow, the birds' surface to volume ratio becomes smaller, reducing this problem.

The best way to provide heat for the young birds is to suspend a reflecting-style heat lamp dome over part of their pen. The lamp should be high enough that it will not become wet or covered in dust, paper or straw. This is very important – a drop of cold water can make a hot light bulb explode. Usually, the lamp should be mounted about 18-inches from the floor.

Use a red bulb so that the light does not disturb the ducks during the night. Experiment with different wattages until the temperature under the lamp is about 90 to 95 degrees Fahrenheit. Use a digital thermometer to monitor the temperatures.

When suspending the light bulb, place it so that it only illuminates a portion of the pen. This will allow the ducklings to move out of the light when they attain suitably high temperatures. It is easiest to do this by placing the heat lamp at one end of the enclosure; but you can also accomplish this by suspending the light in the center of the pen, if there is sufficient space outside of the lit area for the ducks to rest. However, this may force the ducklings to split up, so it is best to place it at one end. This creates a natural thermal gradient, which allows the ducks access to a wide range of temperatures.

While you should measure the temperatures of the pen regularly, consider the behavior of the ducks as well. If the ducks are always huddled under the heat lamp, they are not warm enough. In contrast, if they are usually avoiding the heat lamp, the heat lamp may be too warm. Pay attention to what the ducks are telling you, and alter their temperatures accordingly.

Each week, you can lower the temperature of the heat lamp by about 5 degrees, though this is not necessary – if the chicks are too hot, they will simply move from under the lamp. After about two or three weeks, you can stop turning the lamp on during the day. After three to five weeks, the light is not necessary at all, even in cool weather.

As they grow, the ducks will become more and more insulated, their surface to volume ratio will shrink and they will be less susceptible to the cold. Although they are a tropical species, the adults acclimate suitably to sub-freezing temperatures, as long as they are able to find somewhere to dry off and get out of the wind – particularly at night.

Water

Mallard ducks enjoy swimming, but they will not develop serious health problems if they are not able to swim. Make no mistake, swimming accommodations are important to ensure that your duck lives a full and enriched life; however, they will not die for lack of swimming water.

However, without fresh water for drinking, ducks will quickly become ill. Death can follow in as little as 24 to 48 hours with no water.

Accordingly, you must make sure that young ducklings always have access to fresh drinking water. The best way to provide this is via a small, shallow dish or with a commercially produced duck water dispenser.

Dishes can be made from glass, plastic or ceramic, but avoid galvanized steel with ducks. When offering water for young ducklings it is important to keep the dish shallow, as baby ducks can drown very easily.

Nipple style water dispensers also work well for ducks, although you may need to show them that the nipples release water.

This water must be kept very clean to prevent the ducks from getting sick. Unfortunately, the ducks often seem determined to make the biggest mess possible. You will have to change the water every day and clean out the dish with soap and water. You can help keep the water cleaner by providing more than one water dish, which will tend to spread the mess over more water.

Once the birds have reached three to five weeks of age, you can start allowing them to swim in very shallow pools. Keep the water less than ½ inch deep until the young ducklings are strong swimmers. Always be sure that the ducks can get into and out of the water very easily.

Over the next several weeks, you can begin transitioning the ducks to their long-term housing protocols. For example, if you plan to move the ducks to an outdoor pond when they mature, you can begin taking them for brief, supervised outings so that they can gradually become accustomed to their future home.

Alternatively, if you plan to herd the ducks, you will need to begin familiarizing them with the daily procedure, while supervising them whenever they are outside.

2. Long-Term Housing

By the time your Mallard ducks are about 12 weeks old, you can treat them as adults. There are several different basic housing options, and each has a nearly infinite capacity for customization.

Water for Swimming?

While Mallard ducks certainly need copious amounts of clean water for drinking, they do not require swimming water for survival. It is true that Mallard ducks are not as aquatic as Mallard-derived breeds, but they appreciate a swimming area that affords them the chance to bathe, swim and forage.

Tens of millions of Mallard ducks are produced each year in commercial operations, and most of these do not provide swimming water for their livestock. However, the goals and ethos of a commercial duck production facility are different from those of a pet owner. A pet owner should always seek to provide their companions with the highest quality of life possible.

If the prospect of providing and maintaining swimming water for the animals is not palatable, perhaps waterfowl are not an ideal pet for you.

With that said, offering your pets swimming water for several hours, two or three times a week may be a sufficient compromise. In some respects, this approach may even be better for the ducks' long-term well being.

Given a small flock of three or four Mallard Ducks, a large child's plastic wading pool may be large enough to give the birds the exercise they need. Such a swimming pool can be emptied, cleaned and re-filled between uses to ensure clean water. The lack of swimming water will also prevent a great deal of the mess that the ducks will create as they drag water all over the enclosure, creating mud.

Simplest Enclosure Possible

Often, the best way to house ducks – particularly for new keepers – is the simplest way possible. This means eliminating any unnecessary components of the enclosure and providing only the things that the ducks require to remain healthy and happy.

To accomplish this, provide your Mallard ducks with a small, enclosed, outdoor pen with a large, permanent water container. A small child's swimming pool or stock tank can be added to the enclosed space to provide swimming opportunities. In the interest of simplicity, it is best to fill the pool periodically, rather than leaving it full all of the time. Be sure to flip the pool upside down when not in use to prevent the ducks from falling in and injuring themselves.

In principle, such a pen features several wooden posts and some material to form the pen's walls (and roof, if so desired). It is possible to use existing structures as a portion of the enclosure. For example, if the pen is constructed next to a building, one of the building's exterior walls can serve as one of the enclosure's walls.

Many different materials can be used to make the enclosure's walls. Chicken wire and similar metal mesh products are popular choices. When possible, plastic-coated wires should be used, as they are less likely to cause injury.

Alternatively, the walls of the pen can be made from corrugated plastic panels, wood that has been sealed for outdoor use, or cement. Poured cement walls are hard to beat in terms of durability, but building such walls is a significant undertaking.

Be sure that the gaps in the fence are either small enough to prevent the ducks from poking their heads through the holes at all or large enough that they can poke their heads through and retract them without becoming stuck. Always ensure that there are no exposed sharp edges or rough surfaces when attaching the metal material to the supports.

While such pens need not be expansive, it must be large enough to allow the ducks enough space for exercise and personal space. Two to four ducks will live happily in a pen with approximately 100 square feet (9.36 square meters) of space.

The simplest floors to maintain are made of smooth concrete. By pouring the floor at a gentle slope, the floor can be hosed down and kept clean with ease. However, pouring a concrete floor is a significant undertaking that may be beyond the skill set or budget for one keeping a few pet ducks.

If concrete floors are impractical, several other choices are possible. Wood shavings or mulch make a suitable ground cover, although they will require frequent replacement. Additionally, you must be sure that the wood chips are not sharp or too rough, as they may injure your ducks' delicate feet.

Grass, clover or similar ground covers are suitable, although it is more difficult to keep this area clean. The duck's droppings will biodegrade over time, but in a small enclosure, their waste will build up more quickly than it will degrade. The only viable approach for small, grass-floored pens is to remove droppings manually, once or twice per week.

In addition, the enclosure will require some type of shelter or roost in which the ducks can sleep and retreat from inclement weather.

A variety of different shelters are possible, from elaborate, custom-built shelters, made from wood and screws, to simple, plastic doghouses. The shelter must be large enough for the ducks to extend their wings and have enough personal space to avoid causing stress and infighting – especially if the ducks are forced to remain in the shelter overnight.

Raised Pens

Instead of constructing a pen directly on the ground, it is possible to build a raised pen for your Mallard ducks. Raising the pen off the ground entails a great deal more effort in terms of designing and constructing the enclosure, but the benefits of a raised pen are substantial.

Usually, such pens are constructed by building a wooden frame, and then enclosing the area as with a standard pen, by using some type of metal mesh. By raising the cage off the ground, the ducks' droppings will pass through the floor of the pen onto the ground below. While the keeper will still be forced to contend with the copious droppings, they will not remain in contact with the ducks. This helps to ensure that the ducks stay healthy and clean. In addition, spilled drinking or swimming water will not saturate the ground, causing a muddy mess inside the cage.

Additionally, because such pens are elevated, it is possible to plumb a swimming pool, which will allow easy filling and draining. By cutting a hole in the bottom of a small stock tank or children's wading pool, you can attach PVC fittings and pipes that will serve as a drain. If the piping is sized to fit a hose, the soiled water can be drained and used to water lawns or ornamental plants in other parts of the yard.

It is generally easy to mount the swimming pool flush with the floor by cutting a hole in a section of the mesh floor, and constructing a frame of wood around the hole to support the lip or rim of the pool.

Raised pens require a shelter as well. The easiest way to provide one is by covering the roof and three walls of one end of the cage to create a covered alcove. In particularly cold climates, it may be advisable to use a solid floor for the cage to reduce drafts that come up through the floor.

One of the greatest benefits of raised pens is that it is easy to fill and drain the swimming pool. Additionally, raised pens do not become muddy, and keep your ducks cleaner than pens built on the ground. Finally – and most importantly for some keepers – raised pens are very secure from many predators. However, these benefits are offset to some degree by the cost and labor involved in constructing a pen suitably sized for such large ducks.

While many keepers – particularly small-scale breeders – use raised pens for young ducks, relatively few keepers use raised pens for adult Mallard Ducks. This is due in part to the ducks' large size. At a minimum, the pen should have approximately 100 square feet (9.36 square meters) of space, and be a minimum of 30 to 36 inches ((75 to 100 centimeters) high.

Such large structures may not be permissible in some residential areas, or they may require expensive construction permits to erect. Additionally, some may consider them to be an eyesore unless constructed in such a way to be aesthetically pleasing.

Free Range

If you are blessed to have a large amount of land, you may elect to keep your ducks in a free-range manner. To do so, the ducks are allowed to roam as they wish, although it is advisable to use a fence around the perimeter of the property to prevent the ducks from wandering off.

This is a very rewarding way of housing your ducks, but it requires a large space, considerable effort to "duck-proof" the area and is the least secure method for housing your beloved pets.

When keeping your ducks out in the open, hawks and owls are an ever-present threat to your pets, even if a perimeter fence excludes dogs, coyotes and foxes.

The relative risk to adult Mallard Ducks is modest, but young ducklings are very vulnerable to hawks and owls. There are ways to reduce the risk further, such as employing the services of a guard or herding dog. While far from infallible, few birds of prey will venture too close to a large canine.

Free-range ducks must have a suitable enclosure for sleeping and avoiding bad weather and predators.

Often, free-range housing is used to take advantage of an existing pond or water feature. This provides the ducks with a wonderful resource for swimming, bathing, escaping terrestrial predators and foraging. Additionally, if of sufficient size, such naturally occurring ponds are unlikely to become polluted from two to four ducks. For larger flocks, care must be taken to ensure the ducks' droppings do not overwhelm the pond's flora and fauna.

Free-range keeping of Mallard Ducks should only be conducted if you own or have rights to the entire area to which they have access. In other words, do not attempt to keep Mallard ducks in a free-range manner in a large reservoir that connects to different properties. Not only could the ducks be injured by pets or unsupervised children, but your neighbors may not appreciate your pets' droppings on their manicured lawns.

Keeping your Mallard Ducks in a free-range system means that they may fly away if their wings have not been pinioned or clipped. However, if the ducks have plentiful food, water and shelter, they are unlikely to leave the area.

Herding

Many keepers employ a modified free-range technique. Called "herding," the technique is largely similar to free range keeping, but the ducks are herded into a dedicated sleeping shelter at night. Once inside their sleeping quarters, the ducks are locked in securely. The next morning, the ducks are herded back to their activity area.

Herding drastically reduces the chances of predation at night, yet still allows the ducks daily access to natural forage and swimming opportunities. Additionally, by having two different activity zones for the ducks (the daytime activity area and the sleeping quarters), you can tend to one while the ducks are in the other. This is easier for the keeper, and less stressful for the kept.

Constructing a Pond from Scratch

If you would like to provide your ducks with a small pond, but do not have an existing pond on your property, you can build one from scratch. Understand that such an endeavor is a significant undertaking that is likely to cost several thousand dollars to complete; however, constructing such a pond provides a number of benefits for your companions.

Typically, the best location for a pond is at a low-lying area, where water already accumulates. Through the course of digging out the pond, you will likely produce enough fill dirt to construct the necessary dams or berms, which funnel the water to the pond.

Before setting out to construct your own pond, you must research the permits necessary for your area. Additionally, you will need to contact your local extension service to find out the water-retention properties of your local soil. In general, clay soils are better for holding water than sandy or loamy soils are.

Additionally, you must find out the appropriate amount of watershed area that is necessary to keep a pond filled in your area.

For example, in the Eastern United States, where rainfall is plentiful, ten or fifteen acres of watershed land may keep a 1-acre pond full to a depth of 3 to 5 feet. In contrast, in the arid west, it may take hundreds of acres of watershed land to keep a 1-acre pond this full.

It is also important to ensure that the pond can accommodate floods so as not to harm the property of your neighbors at lower elevations.

Adapting an Existing Pond

Of course, it is easier to provide a pond for your ducks if you already have one on your land. However, depending on the prior use of the pond, it may not be ready for ducks.

It is important to ensure that the pond does not have any submerged objects that may injure or ensnare the birds. This includes sunken boats, trash, construction materials and lost fishing lures or string. Fishing line and tackle are especially dangerous items to have in duck ponds. The ducks often eat lead weights, as they look similar to nuts or seeds. This can cause them to develop lead poisoning. Fishing line can ensnare them badly enough that they never break free. If the fishing line is under the water, it may also cause the ducks to drown.

Additionally, the pond must be easy for the ducks to enter and exit. The best option is to construct a gently sloping beach if one does not already exist. The ducks may be able to scale shores successfully if they are built from riprap or large boulders, but the rough surfaces may abrade the ducks' delicate feet. Additionally, riprap provides excellent places for predators, such as snakes and minks, to hide.

The pond will likely support more forage if it has abundant plant life. While you should be able to access all portions of the pond, some portions of the pond-land interface should have ample vegetation on the land and in the water.

You can stock the pond with turtles, fish and frogs if you wish, but their impact on the water chemistry must be taken into account. In general, the more animals that are present, the more vegetation is necessary. The vegetation will use much of the ammonia produced by the animals, and oxygenate the water.

Ponds that are in direct sunlight for the bulk of the day will tend to suffer from higher algae blooms and an increased rate of evaporation. However, ponds that receive direct sunlight are less likely to freeze than shaded ponds are.

Depending on the flora and fauna you intend to stock the pond with, the depth of the water will have to account for local weather conditions. For example, a pond in the southern United States may not be at risk of freezing, so great depth is not necessary to prevent fish, turtles or frogs from dying off in the winter. In contrast, a pond in western Canada must be very deep to prevent killing fish or frogs in the winter.

For those living in cold climates, it may not be feasible to provide the ducks with swimming water year-round. This will not harm their health, but they must be given regular access to drinking water.

Predator-Proof Checklist

Many different animals view your beloved pets as a tempting and tasty snack. While it is very difficult to eliminate this possibility, most keepers are keen to reduce these odds as much as possible. Ultimately, the keeper will have to decide the level of risk they are willing to take on behalf of their birds.

Hatchling Mallard Ducks are at the greatest risk to predators. Their small size means that a greater number of animals are capable of consuming them and their inexperience makes them less prepared to avoid predators. Hatchling and juvenile Mallard Ducks are at risk of the following predators:

Large snakes

Hawks

Owls

Ravens

Crows

Magpies

Kestrels

Dingoes

Falcons

Raccoons

Opossums

Foxes

Coyotes

Bobcats

Weasels

Minks

Otters

Herons and other large wading birds

Large turtles

Crocodilians

Skunks

Rats

Badgers

Wolverines

Ferrets / pole cats

Domestic Dogs

Domestic Cats

Bears

Large predatory fish

Large amphibians, particularly frogs

Additionally, keepers who reside in tropical regions must contend with large lizards, primates and other ground-based predators, such as mongooses.

By virtue of their large size, adult Mallard Ducks are not at risk of many of the predators that can consume young ducks. Additionally, their life experience helps them to avoid many predators by swimming or flying away. However, the adults are still at risk of:

Large Hawks

Large Owls

Foxes

Coyotes

Dingoes	Crocodilians
Domestic Dogs	Bobcats
Domestic Cats	Bears
Wolverines	Raccoons
Badgers	

Additionally, in areas where such predators exist, very large snakes, lizards, primates or cats may also prey upon ducks.

When constructing your outdoor pen, consider the following questions:

- Are the ducks protected from untrustworthy and unknown canines?

- Are the ducks protected from domestic or feral cats, raccoons, opossums, weasels and other climbing and digging predators?

- Are the ducks protected from birds of prey? This is important during the day (hawks) and at night (owls).

- Are the ducks protected from small animals, such as rats and snakes?

- Are the ducks protected from malevolent Homo sapiens?

- Are the ducks protected from aquatic predators, such as large fish, turtles and crocodilians?

You can also experiment with anti-predator devices, as long as they do not frighten the ducks. For example, a scarecrow may dissuade crows and small hawks. Predator decoys, such as plastic owls, may discourage rats, snakes and other small animals from hunting your young ducks.

Decoys that move – such as when they are blown by the wind – are more effective than completely stationary ones. If this is not possible, consider moving the decoy regularly. Other techniques, such as sprinkler systems and noise-making devices may dissuade terrestrial predators, such as foxes and dogs.

Do not use commercial chemical repellants to keep predators away from your ducks. Such chemicals rarely work, and often have harmful components. Remember that your ducks' pond is at the bottom of your local watershed, and anything that is poured on the surrounding land will usually wash into the water.

Ultrasonic noise producers and similar devices should be avoided as well. They may irritate your ducks and keep much of their insect prey from venturing into the area.

Some duck keepers place predator traps along the periphery of the property in hopes of reducing the local population. Usually, this is an exercise in futility, as it is very difficult to consistently trap predators.

Even if you manage to catch one or two predators, the other ones in the area are just as likely to stay close by, and devour your precious ducklings at a later date. Many intelligent predators – especially dogs, foxes and coyotes – learn to recognize and avoid traps very quickly.

Traps can be dangerous to ducks and humans as well as predators, so you must weigh the potential protective value of the traps versus the potential for injuring one of your ducks or children. Additionally, if you are successful in trapping the predator, you will be faced with an injured, frightened animal that must be humanely euthanized. Such procedures exceed the capabilities and skill of casual duck owners.

Trapping regulations vary widely from one location to the next, so be sure to check with your local officials to avoid conflicting with the law.

Depending upon the type of predator that you are dealing with, you may take necessary precautions. For instance, if you have to deal with a Bobcat that is threatening the safety of your ducks, you can also bring home a dog that will be able to safeguard your ducks. If you have had attacks during the day, you may also hire someone to supervise the space for a while. When predators are aware of the supervision, they will strike less often.

The biggest mistake that you can make with predators is providing them with space to hide. If there are large sacks or cans, you must get rid of them immediately. Predators like coyotes love to hide, watch and then attack. If their hiding spaces are eliminated, even the attacks will reduce significantly.

The other important precaution for duck owners is to ensure that there is no garbage that is out in the open. This prevents predators such as raccoons who come in primarily to get some food. Then, they end up attacking your precious pets.

If you feel like none of your precautions are working, you may also contact your Local Environment Council. They will be able to provide you with the right methods of controlling the most prolific predators.

Chapter 8: Feeding Your Pet Duck

Feeding your duck properly is more complicated than simply tossing a few pieces of bread into their pen each day. You must ensure that you offer them the right types of food, a diverse variety of food and that you offer it at the proper frequency.

1. Food

Ideally, pet Mallard ducks have the opportunity to eat several different types of food. In addition to commercially produced food and the occasional table scrap, Mallard ducks should always have the ability to consume natural forage as well.

Natural Forage

One of the most important aspects for both keeping your pets healthy and maximizing the benefits they offer is ensuring that they forage for natural foods. Wild and range-reared Mallard ducks consume an amazing amount of insects, spiders, tick, slugs and snails. These foods are an important – and free – component of the species' diet. Some farmers keep a flock of Mallard ducks simply for their pest control contributions.

In northern latitudes, Mallard Ducks may be more inclined to consume insects in the afternoon, once the land has warmed sufficiently. Mallard Ducks living in warmer climates may forage for insects earlier in the day.

In addition to insects and other invertebrates, Mallard Ducks also consume a large amount of grass and herbaceous vegetation. If the size of the flock is in balance with the size of the area, the ducks can keep a lawn reasonably well trimmed. Mallard Ducks also consume fruits, whether they find them on the ground or attached to the plant.

Because they may harm plants in pursuit of their creepy-crawly prey, some keepers find it necessary to confine the ducks' activities or protect sensitive plants with fencing.

Commercially Prepared Foods

Commercially prepared duck chow should form the bulk of your ducks' diet. In an ideal scenario, your ducks would obtain all of their food by foraging, but this may lead them to stray from your yard if they are not completely contained or if they have not had their wings clipped or pinioned.

Accordingly, the best idea for most keepers is to provide enough commercial food to keep the ducks well fed and happy to hang around, but not so much that they lose interest in foraging.

Creating food for ducks and other poultry is a multi-billion dollar industry. Accordingly, a wide variety of feed is available, each tailored to a different type and age of duck. Additionally, these foods are often specifically designed for birds that are being raised for meat, egg production or as pets.

In general, growing chicks require a significant portion of protein in their diet to fuel the construction of new body tissues. As they grow, their protein needs gradually decline.

Some duck breeders feed their ducks high-protein foods until they mature and begin to lay. In some cases, this food may be composed of up to 28 percent protein.

Egg-laying females require extra calcium to produce eggshells. Many foods for laying hens contain up to 20 percent protein.

Most breeders recommend switching from a high-protein "starter" food to a "breeder" food, with lower protein, at about three to five weeks of age.

It is important that you do not offer chicken food to ducks. Many chicken foods contain medication that will make your Mallard Ducks sick. Some duck keepers and breeders seek to mix their own feeds. This is often necessary if you cannot find the correct protein percentage for your ducks.

If you are not sure which type of food to offer your Mallard Ducks, consult your veterinarian. Alternatively, the breeder from whom you purchased the birds may be able to suggest the proper food for your pets.

Other Dietary Items

It is usually acceptable to offer your Mallard Ducks table scraps on occasion. Avoid greasy, salty foods.

Fruits

Blackberries

Blueberries

Raspberries

Cranberries

Boysenberries

Loganberries

Pear (sliced or cubed)

Squash (sliced or cubed)

Pumpkin (cubed)

Apple (sliced of cubed)

Papaya (sliced of cubed)

Grapes (sliced)

Pineapple (cubed)

Watermelon (cubed)

Sweet peppers (sliced)

Eggplant (cubed)

Peaches (sliced or cubed)

Cucumber (sliced or cubed)

Figs (sliced)

Persimmons (sliced)

Cantaloupe (cubed)

Vegetables

Collard greens (cut)

Spinach (only in moderation)

Romaine lettuce (cut)

Radicchio (cut)

Carrots (shredded or cubed)

Broccoli (cut into small pieces)

Cabbage (cut)

Cauliflower (cut into small pieces)

Asparagus (cut)

Kale (cut)

Beets (cut)

Most sprouts

Grains, Legumes and Seeds

Cracked corn

Popcorn

Wheat

Barley

Oats

Rice

Milo

Peas

Cooked green beans (cut)

Cooked snow peas (cut)

Cooked lima beans

Cooked black beans

Cooked pinto beans

Sunflower seeds

Safflower seeds

Sesame seeds

Pumpkin seeds

Mixed birdseed (no Peanuts)

Many plants that grow in your yard are acceptable food for Mallard ducks. Always be sure that toxic chemicals, such as fertilizers, pesticides or insecticides, are not used in areas where your ducks feed.

Dandelion

Clover

Bermuda grass

Winter rye grass

Fescue grass	Wintergrass
Centipede grass	Wheat grass
Zoysia grass	Crab grass
Rye grass	Tall oat grass
Blue grass	Orchard grass
Kikuyu grass	Grape leaves
Blue Grama grass	
Dallas grass	

Additionally, there are a variety of live animals that you can supplement your ducks' diet with.

Crickets	Moths
Mealworms	Leaches
Superworms	Grasshoppers
Wax worms	Roaches
Silk worms	Guppies
Earthworms	Minnows
Nightcrawlers	Shad
Red Wigglers	Goldfish

2. Frequency

Ducks need to eat every day. Ideally, your ducks will consume a varied diet, including commercially produced food, fruits and vegetables, and worms and other small feeders you provide. Additionally, your Mallard Ducks should consume a large amount of wild grasses, insects and other items as well.

Many keepers help encourage their Mallard Ducks to forage by providing them with commercial food in the afternoons. Others choose to simply feed their ducks each day, and allow them to eat the commercial diet when they choose.

Others leave food out at all times. While this is an acceptable strategy, you must be sure to keep the feeding containers clean. Do not simply pour new commercial food on top of the uneaten food in the food dish.

Always be sure that the ducks have access to water whenever food is present. Otherwise, the ducks could have trouble swallowing their food and they may choke.

3. Things to Avoid

Unless directed by your veterinarian, avoid medicated duck feeds. Improper use of such foods can cause lameness or death.

Do not feed your ducks bread. While bread is not toxic to birds, it is a very poor food source. Packed with sugar and calories, but very little else, bread takes up a lot of room in the ducks' digestive tract, without offering any substantial nutrition.

Additionally, ducks love to eat bread, and will often do so while forsaking all other foods. Bread can take up space in the ducks' esophagus or gizzard, potentially blocking them and causing further problems.

Spinach and other vegetables that are high in oxalic acids are not toxic to ducks, but they should only be fed in moderation. Such vegetables bind with the calcium in the ducks' diets, leading to deficiencies – this is especially problematic for laying females.

Onions are toxic to birds. Garlic, shallots and chives should also be avoided as they are similar and may cause serious health problems. Prolonged exposure to onions can cause birds to develop a condition known as hemolytic anemia.

Chocolate is toxic to many animals, including Mallard ducks. If the birds eat chocolate, it can cause them to experience significant digestive disorders. Serious cases involving chocolate poisoning can cause nervous system problems, convulsions and death.

Avocados are incredibly toxic to birds. All parts of the plant can cause fatal heart problems for your ducks.

Avoid feeding your ducks processed foods. This includes canned vegetables and processed carbohydrates. Such foods are invariably high in salts, fats and sugars. Although they are not technically toxic, these substances can cause serious health problems for your ducks in surprisingly small quantities.

Ducks swallows nuts whole, and if too many are consumed, they can fill the esophagus, causing digestive problems. While some wild ducks routinely eat acorns, it is best to err on the side of caution. Additionally, most nuts have a high fat content, which is not ideal for the ducks.

Citrus fruits are simply too acidic for ducks. Avoid oranges, lemons, limes and grapefruit.

While unsalted and unbuttered popcorn does not represent a health hazard from a nutritional standpoint, the shape and texture of the food can cause problems. Ducks often get the popcorn stuck in their throat, where it can cause abrasions and wounds.

Potentially Toxic Plants

Little research has been performed to determine which plants, if any, are toxic to ducks. In general, Mallard Ducks are not likely to experience health problems from eating toxic plants. Whether this is due to natural immunity or aversion to toxic species remains unknown.

It is wise to inspect the area in which the ducks will spend time and learn which plants are in the area. A small field guide to the herbaceous plants in your area should help you identify any unknown species. Your local agricultural extension office is also a valuable resource for learning about local plants.

The following chart contains many of the plants that either are known to be toxic to ducks, or are known to be toxic to other animals, such as cat and dogs:

Common Name	Scientific Name
Amaryllis	*Amaryllis belladonna*
Anemone	*Anemone* sp.
Anthurium	*Anthurium* sp.
Asparagus Fern	*Asparagus sprengerii*
Arrowhead Vine	*Syngonium podophyllum*
Atamasco Lily	*Zephyranthes* sp.
Azalea	*Rhododendron sp.*
Autumn Crocus	*Colchicum autumnale*
Avocado	*Persea americana*
Baneberry	*Actaea* sp.
Begonia	*Begonia* sp.
Bird of Paradise	*Poinciana gilliesii*
Black Cherry	*Prunus serotina*
Black Locust	*Robinia pseudoacacia*
Black Nightshade	*Solanum nigrum*
Black Snakeroot	*Zigadenus* sp.
Bleeding Heart	*Dicentra spectabilis*
Bloodroot	*Sanguinaria canadensis*
Boxwood	*Buxus* sp
Boston Ivy	*Parthenocissus tricuspidata*

Buttercup	*Ranunculus* sp.
Butterfly Weed	*Asclepias* sp.
Caladium	*Caladium* sp.
Calla Lily	*Zantedeschia* sp.
Candytuft	*Iberis* sp.
Cardinal Flower	*Lobelia cardinalis*
Carolina Jasmine	*Gelsemium sempervirens*
Castor Beans	*Ricinus communis*
Cherry Laurel	*Prunus caroliniana*
Chinaberry	*Melia azedarach*
Christmas Rose	*Helleborus niger*
Clematis	*Clematis* sp.
Coriander	*Coriandrum sativum*
Corn Cockle	*Agrostemma githago*
Cowslip	*Caltha palustris*
Daffodil	*Narcissus* sp.
Delphinium	*Delphinium* sp.
Elderberry	*Sambucus* sp.
English Ivy	*Hedera helix*
Four O'clock	*Mirabilis jalapa*
Foxglove	*Digitalis purpurea*
Giant Elephant Ear	*Alocasia* sp.

Gloriosa Lily	*Glonosa superba*
Golden Chain Tree	*Labunum anagryroides*
Goldenseal	*Hydrastis canadensis*
Henbane	*Hyoscyamus niger*
Holly	*Ilex* sp.
Horse Chestnut	*Aesculus* sp.
Hyacinth	*Hyacinthus orientalis*
Hydrangeas	*Hydrangea* sp.
Ivy (Common / English)	*Hedera helix*
Irises	*Iris* sp.
Jack-In-The-Pulpit	*Arisaemia triphyllum*
Jerusalem Cherry	*Solanum pseudocapsicum*
Junipers / Red Cedars	*Juniperus* sp.
Lilly of the Nile	*Agapanthus africanus*
Lilly of the Valley	*Convallaria* sp.
Lobelia	*Lobelia* sp.
Lucky Nut	*Thevetia peruviana*
Lupine	*Lupinus* sp.
Marijuana	*Cannabis* sp.
Meadow Buttercup	*Ranunculus acris*
Milkweed	*Asclepias* sp.
Mistletoe	*Viscum* sp.

Mock Orange	*Philadelphus* sp.
Mountain Laurel	*Kalmia latifolia*
Mourning Glory	Family *Convolvulaceae*
Nandina	*Nandinaa domestica*
Nightshades	*Solanum* sp.
Parsley	*Petroselinum crispum*
Periwinkle	*Vinca minor* and *V. major*
Philodendron	*Philodendron* sp.
Pittosporum	*Pittosporum* sp.
Poinsettia	*Euphorbia pulcherrima*
Potato Plants	*Solanum tuberosum*
Pothos	*Pothos* sp.
Primrose	*Primula* sp.
Privet	*Ligustrum* sp.
Rapeseed	*Brassica napus*
Rhubarb (leaves)	*Rheum rhabarbarum*
Rosary Bean	*Abrus precatarius*
Schefflera	*Schefflera* sp.
Shasta Daisy	*Chrysanthemum maximum*
Sorghum	*Sorghum* sp.
Spider Mum	*Chrysanthemum morifolium*
Split Leaf Philodendron	*Monstera deliciosa*

Spring Adonis	*Adonis vernalis*
St. John's Wort	*Hypericum perforatum*
Strawberry Bush	*Euonymous* sp.
Tobacco	*Nicotiana* sp.
Trumpet Flower	*Solandra* sp.
Umbrella Tree	*Schefflera actinophylla*
Water Hemlock	*Cicuta maculata*
Weeping Yew	*Taxus* sp.
Wisteria	*Wisteria* sp.

Source: www.allthedirtongardening.com

This list is not exhaustive. If you are concerned about plant species that are not on this list, check with your local poison control center or veterinarian for more information.

Grit

When discussing ducks, the term grit refers to fine sand and small rocks that partially fill the duck's gizzard. This material functions similarly to the teeth of other animals. The gizzard – technically called the ventriculus - is a muscular organ that helps to digest their food. To improve the performance of the organ, ducks swallow grit and then carry it in their gizzard.

The gizzard is a very interesting organ, and it is capable of changing its size in response to the food the duck is eating. For example, ducks that routinely consume foods hard to digest usually exhibit enlarged gizzards. Those that consume softer plants and fruits have more modestly sized gizzards.

You must provide some type of grit for your ducks so that they can digest their food properly. If your ducks are kept outdoors and have access to a variety of sands and mud, they will find their own grit. However, if they are kept in concrete-floored pens, or are otherwise unable to find grit themselves, you will have to supply them with supplemental grit.

Grit is available at many of the same places that sell duck feed. Do not place the grit directly on the duck's food. Instead, provide the grit in a separate bowl and allow them to swallow the grit as necessary.

Oyster Shell

Crushed oyster shell is a calcium-rich supplement that some duck keepers like to provide their ducks. However, care should be taken to ensure that non-laying females and drakes are unable to eat significant amounts of oyster shell.

Oyster shell is provided to offset the calcium demands that the females experience during egg laying. Females that do not have sufficient dietary calcium will produce thin-shelled or pitted eggs. Weak eggs are less likely to hatch than those that are properly calcified. In extreme cases, calcium deficiencies can lead to egg binding.

Do not place the oyster shell powder on top of the ducks' food. Instead, place it in a small container and allow the ducks to eat it as they wish.

Instead of crushed oyster shell, some keepers place broken cuttlebone pieces in a dish for their ducks. Cuttlebone is another good source of calcium, but you must ensure that it is broken into small enough pieces.

Excess calcium can cause nearly as many problems as a deficiency can. Kidney disease often follows excess calcium intake. Accordingly, the best way to proceed is to provide your ducks with a healthy, varied diet that includes plenty of foraged greens. Many grasses and other wild-growing plants have a considerable amount of calcium.

If you are in doubt about the proper amount of calcium to provide your ducks, consult your veterinarian. Because calcium-related problems are hard to treat, an ounce of prevention, in this case, is really worth a pound of cure.

4. The Importance of Freshness

It is of paramount importance that only fresh, non-spoiled food is provided to your ducks. Molds and fungi can develop on commercial foods as well as raw fruits and vegetables.

Always be careful to purchase food from a reliable retailer and keep the bag sealed tightly between uses. Do not purchase duck food from questionable sources, and always be wary of foods that have drastically reduced prices. Often, retailers mark down the price of commercial animal foods as they approach their expiration date.

Do not purchase very large bags if you only have a few ducks; the small savings will not be helpful if you cannot feed the food before it expires. Try to keep and store the food in the bag it is packaged in, but if you must transfer it, always mark the container with the food's expiration date. Discard any unused food afterwards (Hilary S. Stern, 2014).

Use common sense when storing fresh fruits, vegetables or "people food." Do not offer your ducks anything that you would not feel comfortable eating yourself. Anything that is slimy, molded, discolored or foul smelling should be discarded.

Fresh fruits and vegetables can be placed in sealed containers and then frozen for future use. Freezing will greatly extend the length of time that the food will stay suitable, but it may compromise the nutritional value slightly.

Chapter 9: Interacting with Your Pet Duck

Mallard ducks have a reputation for being slightly pugnacious, in comparison to some of their mallard-derived relatives. While some Mallard Ducks can be defensive, proud animals that use their size to their advantage, many properly raised Mallard Ducks become loving companions.

Mallard ducks do not like being picked up, and they will take great lengths to discourage you from trying to do so. Mallard ducks are large birds – especially males – and they can inflict injuries with their sharp toenails. Additionally, their flapping wings and pecking beaks can affect an impressive defense.

To add insult to potential injury, most Mallard Ducks will expel the contents of their cloaca upon being lifted. This semi-liquid mixture is a powerful example of natural chemical warfare, the smell of which would probably be effective in dispersing angry mobs. Even those who have spent their lives working with animals and their accompanying waste often find duck droppings to be particularly foul smelling.

This means that holding Mallard ducks is not something to do regularly (small ducklings are a different matter that will be covered below). Mallard ducks are not rabbits, lap dogs or cats, and they do not feel any urge to snuggle with you – it is important that parents and children understand this at the outset.

Accordingly, it is important to understand the best way to move your ducks and pick them up when necessary. Learning the proper techniques ensures that you and your feathered companions get through such encounters with as little stress as possible.

1. Handling Young Ducklings

During the process of raising young ducks, it will often be necessary to move them from one place to another. Fortunately, for the first few months of their lives, Mallard ducks can be held without great difficulty. They may still defecate when lifted off the ground, but because they are small, it is easier to keep the "yucky end" pointed away from you.

Ornery young ducks may peck at the hand that holds them, but they usually learn that you mean them no harm and stop the behavior with time. While the pecking may be off-putting to youngsters, it is a relatively harmless defense mechanism.

To lift a young duck, grip it firmly but gently by the sides, to keep the young bird from flapping its wings. Very small ducks can be grasped by one hand, while older ducklings may require the use of two hands. Allow the feet to slide between your fingers, or gently fold the legs into your hand.

2. Herding Your Duck

Once they are mature, the best approach to keeping Mallard ducks is to avoid picking them up or otherwise handling them, unless absolutely necessary.

As with moving any animals, the easiest way to do so is to convince them to move themselves. This is not hard with ducks; they are seemingly always on the move. The problem arises when you need to get them to move where you want them to move. Essentially, you must learn to be a "duck herder."

While they will never be accused of being as smart as dogs, dolphins or chimpanzees, Mallard Ducks are surprisingly intelligent, and quick to learn routines. In fact, establishing routines is one of the best ways to make herding an easy task.

Ideally, when you open the bird's safe, secure sleeping quarters early in the morning, the ducks will walk outside and move in a more-or-less straight line to their daytime activity area. They should willingly march through the door and be on their way to eating, drinking, swimming and generally being a duck. You can then – ideally – shut the gate behind them without ever having to put your hands on a duck.

In the late afternoon, they should already be anticipating your arrival at the gate or door, and be ready to make the trek back to their sleeping quarters. Upon reaching the roost, a perfect flock makes its way inside and settles down for the night with very little encouragement necessary.

Ducks largely "go with the flow" so it is very helpful to herd flocks of some size. The ducks will take social cues from their neighbors, reinforcing their tendency to walk where you want them to go.

Begin teaching the ducks these behaviors from a very young age. If you begin training your ducks to move from place to place at a young age, they will be much easier to herd when they are larger. Additionally, by virtue of their small size, the young ducklings are easier to control when this begins.

The easiest way to get your ducks accustomed to moving from one place to the other is to bribe them. For example, the ducks will usually be eager to exit their night roost once morning arrives. However, you will have to encourage them to go where you want them to go.

So, when you open the roost in the morning, move swiftly to the area you want the ducks to come to and lure them to follow with some of their favorite food. After doing this for a few days, they will begin to anticipate the routine and will naturally head to that area. Eventually, you can stop feeding them, once the behavior is the normal routine.

Stragglers who wander off or do not seem to be interested in the tasty treat require different strategies. Usually, ducks will flee when approached, so you can use this to your advantage.

While you are 20 yards (18 meters) or more away, begin circling behind the wandering Mallard, so that the duck is between you and where you want it to go. For example, if the duck were at the center of a watch dial and you want it to go towards the 12 o'clock position, move so that you are standing at the 6 o'clock position.

Slowly start moving towards the duck. Usually, the Mallard will begin to walk away from you, and towards the intended location. If other ducks are still heading in the same direction, it will help accelerate the process. The goal is not to stress, harass or frighten the bird. Rather, through gentle persuasion, get the Mallard duck to do as you wish.

If the duck begins veering off course, adjust your position to keep it between you and the target area. Sometimes it can help to have a long stick or pole when doing so. With the long stick, tap the ground to get the duck back on track.

For example, if the duck begins moving off to the left, put the pole in your left hand. Using the increased reach offered by the stick, extend the tip of the stick past the duck on the left, in order to encourage him to bring his course back to the right. Do not touch the bird with the stick, instead the goal is for the bird to see the stick and move the other way.

Some Mallard keepers employ dogs to herd their birds. This is a wonderful option if you have a dog that is suitable and trustworthy enough for the job. In addition to helping to herd the ducks, the dog will likely dissuade predators to some extent. Well-trained dogs that have bonded with the flock can provide effective security for the ducks.

3. Lifting, Holding, Transporting and Catching Your Duck

Even the tamest Mallard ducks are averse to being lifted from the ground or held. Unfortunately, there are times when you will have to coral, capture and hold your Mallard Ducks to inspect their health or move them.

Try to avoid stressing your birds unnecessarily when catching them. One of the best times to do so is during the night, when they will be slightly disoriented. If it is not possible to do so at night, consider herding the ducks into a room or building in which the lights can be turned off. Leave the lights off for about one hour before entering and trying to lift the animal.

If you are unable to catch your duck (many Mallard Ducks are surprisingly agile and able to sneak away from you no matter how close you get) use the corralling technique to get the job done.

Corralling your duck relies on gently herding it into an area where the walls function as a funnel. You can construct such a funnel with boards or any other barrier.

Once the ducks enter the wide end of the funnel, gently encourage them to travel to the narrow end. By doing so, the bird will become trapped, allowing you to get your hands on them.

4. Lifting Your Mallard

Unlike chickens, which are often lifted by the legs, the legs of ducks are not strong enough to withstand this treatment. Lifting a duck by the legs may result in broken legs or feet.

Instead, to lift your duck, grip it by the body. Approach the bird calmly to avoid startling it or encouraging it to flee. Grab the bird gently by the sides, keeping the wings folded flat against the birds' sides. Once you have the duck lifted off the ground, place one of your hands under the bird and gently grasp the feet. This will reduce the chances of being scratched by the duck's long toenails.

Some prefer to let the duck's feet protrude through the fingers, while others prefer to cup the feet in their hands, folding them up against the duck's body. Either technique will work.

Once the duck's feet are secure, press the duck lightly against your body, allowing your arm to keep one wing pressed flat, while your body contains the other wing. This one-handed style allows your free hand to open and close doors, inspect injuries or any number of other tasks.

When releasing your duck, place it down gently. Dropping your duck roughly can cause them significant injury.

5. Transporting Your Pet

From time to time, you may find it necessary to move your duck. For example, you may be forced to take your duck to the veterinarian; or, if you own a particularly beautiful specimen, a competitive show. Either case requires that you have appropriate travel accommodations for your pet. There are two basic choices of duck-transportation-containers: plastic tubs and wire cages.

Plastic Tubs

Plastic transportation tubs are easy to make, and can often be created from recycled or repurposed materials, making them quite affordable. To transform a tub into a duck-carrier, simply drill several 1-inch holes on the top and sides of the tub to provide ventilation. By placing the holes in this manner, air will be drawn in through the sides and vented out through the holes in the lid.

Place some dry straw at the bottom of the tub to provide comfort and to absorb liquids.

If not properly ventilated, this type of transportation vessel can become very damp and full of polluted air that can make your duck very sick.

Opaque tubs are the best choice, as they will prevent the ducks from seeing the activity outside the container. This can stress them, making them more susceptible to illness. Transparent containers can be used, but they should be covered with a lightweight covering to prevent the ducks from becoming stressed.

Wire Cages

Wire cages are perhaps the most popular choice for transporting ducks. These are available commercially in a variety of styles, sizes and price points. The other primary benefits of wire cages are that they offer plenty of ventilation for the inhabitants, which can make them more comfortable in warm environments. However, the open nature of the cage means that these are messier than plastic tubs and odors, spilled water, food and feces are likely to escape the boundaries of the cage from time to time. In cold weather, such cages cannot be left exposed to the elements for extended periods of time.

Transportation Safety

Regardless of the type of transportation vessel you use, always be sure that the container is securely strapped into your vehicle, by using seatbelts, bungee cords or straps. In addition to keeping your ducks safer in the event of an accident, it will help prevent the container from sliding around – something that can cause you to have an accident in the first place!

Never leave ducks unattended in a hot car. The glass windows create a greenhouse effect, which can cause the internal temperature to rise to dangerous levels very quickly. Ducks can and have died from being left in a hot car.

Avoid playing loud music or driving erratically while chauffeuring your ducks. Ultimately, a car ride can be a very stressful experience for your feathered friends, and you should try to keep the event as stress-free as possible.

Aggressive Males

Sometimes, male Mallard ducks become very aggressive during the breeding season. Fueled by hormones and an instinct to challenge all rivals, drakes occasionally display antagonist behaviors towards their keepers. Drakes of this mindset may run at or even chase people, flap their wings and peck at the "offending" humans.

While usually a small inconvenience that will disappear as the season progresses, these actions can frighten some people. Additionally, the ducks could cause minor injuries, particularly if their feet and long toenails are involved in the altercation.

There are two basic strategies for dealing with this problem. The first is to simply provide the duck with some extra space until his hormones calm down. However, this is not always possible. In such cases, it may be more effective to restrain the bird.

The reason the drake is attacking you is that he sees you as a competing male. A problem that arises from partially imprinting on humans, the best way to correct the behavior is to convince him that you are the dominant male (even if you are a woman), not him.

Do this by refusing to back away from the duck when he charges. You may push him back or even grab his body and hold him to the ground for a few minutes.

Take care that you do not hurt your drake, or stress him unnecessarily. Think of it as a wrestling match, where the goal is to simply get him to give up and look for someone else to pick on (which will often be one of the females).

6. Feather Clipping and Pinioning

Besides providing a completely enclosed habitat, there are only two ways to keep your Mallard ducks from flying away: pinioning their wings or clipping their flight feathers.

Pinioning refers to the removal of the distal segment of the birds' wings. The process renders the birds flightless, and need only be performed once, but it is a very traumatic experience for the duck.

This practice is unpalatable to many duck owners, who find it cruel. Additionally, the practice may be illegal in some areas. If you do decide to pinion your ducks, be sure that a properly qualified veterinarian performs the procedure.

It is best to pinion birds when they are very young, if possible. However, the activity can cause so much stress that some youngsters die shortly after the procedure. Often, breeders will pinion the wings of your ducks before you purchase them for a small fee.

By contrast, clipping a duck's flight feathers is harmless and just as effective at keeping the ducks from flying away. The only down side of clipping feathers, as opposed to pinioning, is that it must be performed every year. An additional benefit of clipping the birds' feathers is that you can perform this procedure yourself.

Have someone knowledgeable about birds demonstrate feather clipping the first time. In principle, the primary flight feathers are cut off with a pair of sharp scissors. Usually, the feathers on one wing are clipped, while the feathers on the other wing are left intact.

By removing just a few feathers, these large and heavy ducks become unable to achieve the necessary lift to fly.

If you do not wish to clip the bird's feathers yourself, most veterinarians and pet stores will provide the service for a small fee.

Some keepers elect to accept the possibility that their birds may fly away, as they do not appreciate the alternative. Another reason that some keepers opt for not pinioning or clipping their duck's wings is that they do not want to "disarm" the birds. This is particularly common among keepers who allow their ducks to live in a free-range manner.

The idea is that if a fox, coyote or other land based predator threatens the ducks, they have a better chance of escaping if they have the ability to fly. Even though large drakes cannot get very far from the ground, intact wings will allow them to move and maneuver much more effectively than those who have had their wings altered.

7. Handling and Hygiene

Like most other animals, ducks can carry germs that can make people sick. Some of these germs do not even make the ducks sick, but they can be very dangerous for people. It is always important to practice good hygiene to reduce the chances of contracting an illness.

Many ducks (and other birds) carry Salmonella bacteria in their digestive system. The bacteria is spread via the fecal-oral route, meaning that ducks pass the bacteria in their feces, where it can eventually make its way into the mouth of another duck.

As the ducks excrete infective spores in their droppings, they find their way onto the duck's feathers, feet and beaks, as well as throughout their habitats. The entire area should be considered to be covered in the bacteria.

If some of the bacteria get on your skin, and then you inadvertently transfer some of it to your mouth, you can get sick. It only takes a few spores to cause the illness, so it can be quite easy to catch.

Accordingly, you must be sure to wash your hands after handling poultry or anything in their enclosure. Use an anti-bacterial soap and warm water. Be sure to scrub the tiny nooks and crannies of your hands, where bacteria are likely to persist. This includes your fingernails and the crevices in your knuckles.

It is a good idea to wash your clothing after interacting with the ducks as well. Some keepers keep a pair of slip-on boots handy for when they must enter the enclosure. This way, they do not have to wash their shoes repeatedly.

Salmonella is usually not very serious for healthy adults. However, young children, the elderly and those with compromised immune systems are extremely susceptible to the disease, and often develop serious complications. In rare cases, death can result.

The most common symptoms of the disease are gastrointestinal upset, abdominal cramps and a high fever. Most healthy adults recover from the disease without medical attention, but antibiotics and supportive care may be necessary for high-risk groups.

With this in mind, the Center for Disease Control and Prevention recommends that all live poultry be kept outdoors, and away from areas where people eat or drink. Furthermore, the CDC advises that children under 5 years of age be prevented from touching live poultry.

According to the CDC, live poultry are one of the most likely ways for people to contract the disease. Since the 1990s, more than 45 different outbreaks of the bacteria have originated from live poultry. These outbreaks have caused more than 220 hospitalizations and five deaths (Centers for Disease Control and Prevention, 2014).

Never, under any circumstances, should you use kitchen or bathroom sinks to wash tools or other accessories that have been in contact with the ducks.

Sometimes, a new bird may have infections that will prove fatal to ducks and other fowl present in your farm or garden. The only way to overcome this is by taking adequate measures to quarantine.

Quarantining requires you to keep the new bird away from the rest of the birds for at least 2 to 3 weeks. During this period, your new bird will require a separate coop or house to ensure that he does not mingle with the birds. Many duck owners neglect quarantining to avoid the expense of an additional coop. However, it is worth the investment considering that the entire existing flock is in danger of infection.

8. Understanding Imprinting

The concept of imprinting is rather interesting. The process of this phenomenon is yet to be explained. Nobody knows what exactly happens in the brain of the duck when an imprint is formed. The first and the strongest type of imprint is the filial imprint.

Filial Imprinting is a certain belief pattern in these ducks. As soon as these birds hatch, the first being that they see is recognized as their mother. If you remember watching baby ducks in the wild or even in films, they follow their mothers around and are very keen on obtaining the attention of their mother. Now, it is not necessary that the mother has to be a duck. If you are the first being that a duck sees upon hatching, it is automatically imprinted in its brain that you are mom. Of course, these ducklings are unable to recognize the face or voice of their imprinted parent. However, they will follow you around and expect you to be their mom.

Now, some of you may think that imprinting might be true in case of dogs and cats or other pets, too. After all, they are equally attached to their owners. However, there is one very distinct difference between other animals and birds like ducks and geese.

No matter how attached a dog or cat is to you, it will always recognize itself as a dog or cat respectively. However, when a duckling forms an imprint, it believes that it is the same creature as its parent. So if the imprint formed is that of a human, a duck will believe that he is human.

Even if there are other ducks present around it, the ducking never sees them as parents. It is possible for the duck to understand that he is not a human but is a duck, when he is around others of his own species. However, the filial imprint is only of the being he saw first. The other ducks are only imprinted as his siblings. He will learn and play with his siblings. However, the beauty of this breed is that he will love his 'mom' the most.

If you are planning to hatch eggs, remember that your responsibility does not end with successfully bringing a duckling into this world. Remember that if the baby sees you first after hatching, you are in for a long-term commitment. You will have to play the role of the duckling's mother. Therefore, if you are planning on incubating and hatching a duck egg to bring home a duckling, there are a few things that you must ask yourself.

Do You Have the Time?

Once the duckling believes that you are mom, you are in this relationship for the long run. This is actually a full time job. You will have to sleep next to the duckling, play with him outdoors, eat with him, ensure that he is warm, console him when he is crying and even learn to speak the language of the ducking. The only possible break you will get is a short time away from the duckling when he is in the hands of a trained and experienced duck sitter.

Do You Have the Patience?

There is no way you can litter box train your pet. They are also not capable of controlling their poop. They will mess up your home. Despite being the parent, you cannot even think of disciplining these babies. Even a gentle flick or smack can injure their delicate bills and bones. You might be tempted to use duck diapers but be assured that your babies will absolutely resent it.

Do You Have the Resources?

Although your duckling thinks he is a human, the truth is that he will grow up to be a fully-grown duck whose needs are just the same as any other duck. You must be able to give him a shelter that is free from predators. It is your job to ensure that he eats well and gets the required healthcare. There are also several additional expenses that you will be responsible for.

If you wish to parent a duckling, you must be completely committed. It is also your responsibility to ensure that your duckling interacts with his own species for breeding purposes in the future. You must have the permission of your neighbors and your landlord to have ducks in your home. Remember that they can be quite noisy. If you have pets at home, you are responsible for the safety of the duckling and your pet.

The concept of filial imprinting is quite adorable. However, the responsibility of the parent is far more than taking care of the bird. There is another important concept known as sexual imprinting that you must also be aware of to ensure that your duck grows up and picks the right mate for himself. Although this seems quite natural in the animal world, the way a duck thinks will bewilder you.

Sexual Imprinting

Sexual imprinting is a very important phenomenon in reproduction and breeding. It is through sexual imprinting that a certain species recognizes the attractive features in an opposite gender of the same species. It is with this understanding of attractive features that the bird picks the right mate when it is mature.

With ducks, sexual imprinting works quite differently. The roots of sexual imprinting lie in filial imprinting. Now, if the duck recognizes another duck as its mom, there lies no issue. However, in case the filial imprint is that of a human, it is a task for the human to help this duckling grow up to recognize his own species as desirable to mate with.

If you are planning to hatch an egg, you must make sure that there are several other ducks that this duckling can grow around. In case this does not happen, the duckling will view the features of the human as attractive. So, there are high chances that he will court other people or even the parent instead of other ducks. He might find his entire species altogether unattractive. Therefore, you must be very knowledgeable about the phenomenon of imprinting.

Chapter 10: Breeding Mallard Ducks

Breeding your Mallard ducks can be a fun and educational way to enjoy your pets, increase the size of your flock, supplement your dinner table with fresh duck eggs or make a little extra money by selling the chicks that result. In fact, given a healthy, mature flock and proper husbandry, your female ducks will deposit eggs, whether you want them to or not.

There Is Not Much to It

Unlike some other exotic pets, Mallard ducks do not require any special pre-breeding conditioning to reproduce successfully. As spring approaches and the length of the daylight increases each day, the females' bodies begin preparing to deposit eggs. If you have a drake present, he will breed the females, producing fertile eggs. However, even if no drake is present, or a drake is present but does not successfully breed the females, the females must deposit their eggs.

The breeding instincts of ducks are strong. If kept in enclosures without suitable mates, ducks often engage in same-sex dominance behaviors that superficially resemble mating activity.

Social Concerns

One of the duck keeper's primary jobs during the breeding season is ensuring that the drake does not wound or stress the females. Drakes can be very aggressive in their breeding advances, so you must watch the females for signs of stress or injury. If you notice some of the females are losing feathers, exhibit wounds on their neck, lose significant weight or show signs of stress (loss of appetite, withdrawal, etc.) separate the male to allow them to recover.

If you house more than one male in the same enclosed space, you must ensure that conflicts between them remain "civilized." While posturing, crest raising and chasing are unlikely to cause significant injury, it is possible for males to injure each other. This is especially important if the drakes are not of the same size or social status. A smaller, weaker male must be able to retreat from the dominant drake.

Normally, males work out their differences without many problems. Subordinate males often form bachelor groups that spend most of their time at the periphery of the flock. However, every situation and animal is different, so it pays to be diligent. Often, visual barriers and ample room are sufficient to diffuse tensions and promote flock harmony. Additionally, it is helpful to ensure that there are at least two females for every drake.

Nesting

As egg deposition time approaches, female Mallard Ducks will begin looking for a suitable nesting location. It is best to provide a proper location that is easy to locate, easy to access and safe for the ducks. Otherwise, the female may deposit the eggs somewhere inappropriate, dangerous or impossible to find.

Wild Mallard females use hollow cavities in trees and logs as egg deposition sites. Keep this in mind when preparing your ducks' nesting boxes.

There are many different ways to construct egg-laying boxes (these boxes are also called brooding boxes, because the female will use the boxes to keep the young warm after they hatch). Some keepers build elaborate wooden boxes, while others repurpose plastic doghouses or barrels. In all cases, the boxes must address the same set of concerns:

• The ducks want somewhere dark, secure and appropriately sized. The larger the box is, the more secure it must feel to the ducks. Accomplish this by blocking as many sight lines as possible.

• The nest box must remain as dry as possible while in use. The mother may track some water into the box, but it should dry as soon as possible. Be sure that the box has some airflow to prevent stagnant conditions and accelerate the drying process.

• It is advantageous to use some sort of small barrier at the entrance to the box, for example, a 2x4 piece of lumber, placed on the ground across the entranceway. This will help keep the nest box clean and help contain the hatchlings as they begin moving about. The barrier should be easy for the mother to cross.

• The egg-laying box can be placed directly on bare ground, grass, concrete or wood shavings. Alternatively, you can use an egg box that contains a connected floor. Place some straw or grass clippings on the ground so that the female can form them into a nest.

• Many keepers find that it is helpful to provide more egg-laying boxes than ducks. This helps to keep the ducks from fighting over locations or choosing to lay their eggs outside of a nest box.

• Place the nest boxes in quiet areas that are easy to access. By placing the nest boxes near large structures, such as buildings or large trees, they will benefit from additional protection from the elements. Additionally, the shade will keep the nesting box more secure.

• It is essentially impossible to protect a nesting box from predators if the birds are housed in a free-range style. Accordingly, some keepers elect to move nesting females to secure pens during the laying season.

• Once the female has found a suitable nesting location, she will form the substrate to her liking and pad the bottom with a carpet of down.

Questions to Ask Yourself

Undoubtedly, raising and breeding ducks is a popular occupation across the globe. There are several individuals who will swear by the large benefits that they reaped by simply rearing ducks and trading their eggs. If you are also considering breeding ducks, you can prepare yourself for a rather lucrative business. However, before you actually start breeding ducks, there are some questions that you may want to ask yourself:

• How will I reap profits from the ducks that I am raising?
• What is the breeding purpose?
• Are there enough funds to take care of the birds?
• Do I need additional manpower to run my breeding business? If yes, can I afford the costs of hiring people?
• How safe will the ducks be from predators?
• Do I need any licenses to breed ducks?
• What certification does my breeding program require?
• Will my neighbors be disturbed?

When you have found the answers to these questions, you will be able to decide if breeding ducks is a good idea for you or not. Rearing ducks is very different from having other pets and you must be entirely equipped to provide your ducks with the right care.

The Advantages of Breeding

Breeding Ducks has picked up as a popular vocation across the globe because of the obvious benefits that are associated with it. Ducks are also preferred over other poultry or several reasons. The advantages of choosing duck breeding are:

- **Ducks are easy to handle:** Unlike other poultry, ducks are less demanding. If you have a flock of ducks, you will notice that they are rather content in the company of one another. Other poultry, however, is attention seeking. They are also extremely sensitive because of which they need extra care.

- **Ducks are not high maintenance:** Other farm fowl and poultry are not as rough and tough as ducks. Usually ducks are immune to avian diseases that easily infect other poultry. While ducks do require a great deal of healthcare, they are not as expensive to maintain as other poultry.

- **Ducks are highly adaptable:** Mallard ducks, especially, are known for their ability to survive in diverse environmental conditions. This makes it a lot easier for the owners who do not have to go out of the way to make the ducks feel comfortable and content.

- **Profits from Eggs:** Breeding ducks is also a lot more lucrative than breeding other poultry. Ducks lay a lot more eggs than poultry like chicken. On an average, a duck will lay around 8 to 10 eggs each day. This means that you will get at least 150 eggs in one single reproduction cycle.

- **Better behaved:** In comparison to other poultry, ducks are much better behaved. They are pleasant to have around the farm. The only time ducks display aggressive behavior is when they are in the middle of a reproduction cycle.

- **Hatchlings are easier to raise:** Taking care of the hatchlings is much easier with ducks as they are more adaptable. So, if you are new to breeding ducks are the more suited option.

Duck breeding is considered ideal if you are new to the whole concept of breeding. Since the demands are lesser with ducks, they make for a great practice run before you move on to other poultry.

Types of Breeding

There are two breeding options that you will come across: Natural Breeding and Selective Breeding.

Depending upon the purpose of your breeding program you may choose between the two types. In case of natural breeding, the In case of natural breeding, the ducks mate with only their own kind. Over several decades, there are modifications in the traits and the features of the offspring depending upon the survival needs. As per Charles Darwin, only the birds with the most suitable features for survival would sustain.

In case of artificial breeding, the breeders will induce desirable characteristics from other species to create hybrids. You may indulge in this type of breeding if your primary purpose is to create ducks for exhibition. When you choose artificial breeding, make sure that you are equipped with all the necessary information. If the breeding is not carried out properly, the mutation could be so severe that the resulting offspring may not even be strong enough to survive.

Chapter 11: Mallard Ducks Eggs

If you are planning to bring home Mallard Ducks in order to gain a profit with the eggs that are laid, you must be well informed about the care required to maintain and collect these eggs. Some of you may also be interested in raising a flock of Mallard Ducks in your backyard. In that case, you must know how to hatch the eggs and take proper care of the hatchlings that are produced. Let us take a close look at all the important facts associated with Mallard Duck eggs.

Appearance of the Egg:

Length: 2 to 2.5 inches or 5 to 6.5 cms

Width: 1.5 to 1.8 inches or 3.9 to 4.5 cms

Description: The egg is usually creamy, grayish or greenish in color. The surface is unmarked.

Nutritional Value:

- Protein per egg: 9.5 gms
- 108-130 calories
- Cholesterol: 619 mg
- Fat: 7.3 gms
- Vitamins B6, B12, A, D, E
- 8 essential amino acids
- Phosphorous and Calcium
- Sulphur
- Zinc
- Potassium

-       Iron

Collecting the Eggs

During the breeding season, each hen will lay about 8 to 10 eggs per day. This means that you will get an average of 150 eggs every year. One thing you need to remember about ducks is that the laying of the egg is not restricted to the nest. For those who are interested in an egg business, this is a matter of utmost concern, as the eggs must be collected immediately after they are laid. If you fail to do this, chances are that the eggs will be damaged before you collect them.

Usually, ducks will lay eggs either late in the night or in the wee hours of the morning. If the duck is still laying eggs, you might want to wait for at least two hours so that the eggs have enough time to roost. When you collect the eggs, make sure you do so in a plastic egg tray. Separate the dirty eggs from the clean ones to make your job easier.

If the eggs you are selecting are particularly meant for incubation, you must also check the weight of the egg. If it is even cracked or molted, you must choose another egg for incubation. Eggs with even the slightest deformities are less likely to develop into hatchlings.

Once the eggs have been collected, the next thing to do is clean them. Remember that there are several microbes on the surface of the egg. If the egg is not sufficiently cleaned, there are chances that they will creep in through the shell to spoil the egg. Make sure you get rid of all the mud and manure using steel wool. You may even wipe the eggs.

Remember, washing the eggs is not an option as the contents can be damaged. Choose fumigation if you think that the egg needs thorough cleaning.

Storage

The next thing to worry about is storage. If you want to incubate the eggs, you need to have a decent number. You must wait until you have a few eggs before you begin the incubation process. It is possible to store the eggs for a maximum of seven days provided that humidity and temperature is controlled. The ideal storage temperature for duck eggs is 13 degrees Celsius when the humidity is maintained at 75%.

Dealing with the Eggs

Soon after the female begins sitting on the nest, she will start to deposit one egg each day. Your next step will depend on your goals.

The simplest course of action is to let nature simply take its course. Leave the mother alone and allow her to brood her eggs and hatchlings as she sees fit. Some mothers will prove to be better mothers than others are, and you may lose eggs or hatchlings along the way.

If you would like to harvest the eggs for eating, you can simply remove the new egg each day. The female may continue depositing eggs for some time this way.

Alternatively, you can remove the eggs once she is done with the laying process. The eggs do not begin developing until the last egg has been deposited.

Other keepers prefer to remove the eggs and incubate them inside. Mallard eggs are somewhat difficult to incubate, but it is possible.

If you do not want to breed the ducks, and you do not care for their delicious eggs, you will need to render them unviable. To do so, wait until the female leaves the nest each day to eat, drink and bathe. While she is gone, shake each egg vigorously, and return it to the nest.

Shaking the egg will rupture the blood vessels inside, preventing the egg from developing into a chick. It is important to return the eggs to the nest after shaking them, or the female will just move to another location and deposit another clutch of eggs.

Mallard eggs are rather large, as would be expected from such large ducks. Mallard Ducks produce eggs that contain about three percent more yolk and one percent more shell mass than those of Mallards.

Some keepers like to place protective structures around brooding females to prevent predators from attacking her or the eggs. While the female will often leave the nest when confronted by a large predator (who will then eat most or all of the eggs) they occasionally stick around and try to defend their nest. When this happens, the females often sustain serious injuries, and may not even succeed in protecting the eggs.

Snakes, weasels, raccoons and dogs are frequent predators of duck eggs. Most will attack the nest at night, so you may consider allowing the mother to have her freedom during the day so that she can get food and water and stretch her legs a bit. Then, shortly before nightfall, you can place some sort of "tent" over the female to provide some protection.

If you find that predators are a frequent problem, you may need to enclose the entire area that holds the breeding females. The only other reasonable course of action is to employ the talents of a well-trained guard dog.

Hatching the Eggs

Usually Mallard Ducks will start laying eggs when they are about 7 months old. They are prolific egg layers and will lay about 150-200 hundred eggs each year. Collecting these eggs and hatching them successfully is a challenge. There are two options for hatching the eggs:

- Natural Incubation
- Artificial incubation

Natural Incubation

Brooding is the process when a female actually sits on the eggs to

117

hatch them. There are some obvious signs that you can look out for when your hen is ready to brood. To begin with, she will stop laying eggs. She will also make a very distinct quacking noise. She also sits on the eggs without budging.

There must not be more than 15 eggs on each nest in order to increase hatchability of the eggs. Once the hen begins to brood, she will provide the eggs with the necessary moisture and heat for the eggs to hatch.

There are some things that you must take care of when you have a broody hen:

• The hen should be kept close to food and water
• The nutritional requirements of the brooding ducks must be taken care of.
• Regularly check the ducks for parasites and also for infections

After the first week of brooding, you must check if the eggs are fertile. All you have to do is hold them up against any bright light. If you are able to see a dark shape in the egg, you can be certain that it is fertile. If the egg is clear, it is infertile.

Artificial Incubation

Mallard Ducks will not become broody if the eggs are collected regularly. In such cases, you must opt for artificial incubation. You can make use of commercial incubators to hatch the eggs. These incubators vary in capacity and most often depend upon fuels like gas or kerosene and even electricity to provide heat. The temperature of the device may be controlled with the help of a thermostat that comes with the incubator. The Mallard Duck egg will take about 28 days to hatch when kept in an incubator.

When you remove the eggs are from storage, ensure that they are kept in room temperature for at least 6 hours before they are transferred in to the incubator. The temperature must be set to 37.5 degree Celsius and must be reduced by 0.2 degrees in case of hatchers.

Humidity must also be maintained perfectly. If it is excessive, the eggs won't be dry enough to hatch. If humidity is less, the eggs will dry too quickly. There are special moisture trays to control humidity. Ideally it should be set at 70% relative humidity.

The eggs in the incubator must be turned everyday to make sure that the contents do not adhere to the shell. Generally, it is recommended that the eggs be turned at an angle of 90 degrees. This process can be made automatic with the help of turning equipment that will turn the eggs every hour.

Make sure you constantly check the egg fertilization by shining a light on them. Fumigation is an important process in artificial incubation. Use a mixture of formalin and potassium permanganate to make sure that harmful bacteria, especially salmonella is completely removed.

Removing the hatch from the Incubator

Prepare a brooder with the required heat source when the eggs are close to the hatching date. The average hatchability in ducks is usually about 70%. The hatch must be transferred to the brooder almost as soon as it the process is complete.

Even if the eggs are hatched by natural incubation, brooders are necessary. When the eggs approach the hatching date, you will see that the hen sits on them for shorter periods of time. The hen will spend maximum time away from the nest.

When the ducklings have hatched, special growers pellets should be given as feed to meet the nutritional requirements. These pellets contain the necessary nutrients and minerals that ensure proper development in the ducklings. When the ducklings are about five weeks old, you can introduce wheat with grit. Grit usually consists of oyster shells and helps provide the roughage necessary to break the food down while digesting.

Should you avoid artificial incubation?

Several breeders prefer natural incubation even though there are no recorded issues with artificial insemination. Sometimes Mallard Ducks may stop brooding. In such cases, you can reintroduce them to nesting and brooding using model eggs and even rocks. Eggs can be incubated naturally using certain breeds of chicken as well. Make sure you check the brooding and mothering history of the chicken that you choose as the brooder.

Will my Duck Stop Laying Eggs?

For those whose primary interest lies in earning through the eggs that are available in the breeding season, this is a matter of great concern. Although Mallard Ducks have been known for their amazing egg laying abilities, there are some occasions when they simply will not produce any eggs. If this occurs, the first thing to do would be taking you Mallard Duck to a waterfowl expert. Most often, reproductive disorders and other health disorders will result in your Mallard Duck not laying any eggs. However, there are several other factors that might have lead to a stop in egg laying:

• **The Age of the Bird**: the number of eggs laid will reduce as the duck ages and may eventually come to a halt.

• **Parasites**: If your duck is suffering from any problem related to parasites and ticks, she might be unable to produce healthy eggs. In some cases, the entire process of egg formation is hindered, leading to a stop in the laying of eggs.

• **Weather Conditions**: Ducks are able to produce eggs only when they have ample warmth. In case the weather is not suitable for your duck to produce eggs you can expect her to be unable to do so.

• **Change in Diet:** If you are contemplating a change in your duck's diet, it must be done gradually. You must also make sure that the duck has enough time until the breeding season to get used to a certain kind of diet. If the nutrition is not adequate or is different from what your duck is used to, there is a hindrance in the production of the egg.

• **New Birds in the Flock:** When you introduce new ducks into the flock, it is a big change for the existing ducks. When ducks interact in a group, they tend to be extremely social and also form a pecking order with the other ducks. When you introduce one or more new ducks, this equation changes. The ducks get severely stressed at time and will stop laying eggs for some time until this pecking order has been re-established.

• **Change in Routine:** Ducks are highly disciplined creatures. They need to be fed at a certain time and must also be allowed to roost at a certain time. However, if you make any significant change in any part of their routine, it leads to severe stress, making them stop laying eggs.

• **Improper Husbandry**: If the pen is unclean or overcrowded, the number of eggs laid will reduce significantly. In addition to that, if the conditions of the pen are too dark or cold, it results in stress and illness. As a result, egg laying is reduced considerably and may even stop if poor conditions persist.

• **Too Much Handling**: If you need to transport your birds, you must do it very carefully. During the transfer, they should not be handled too much or handled roughly. Laying is hindered if the transfer is stressful. In addition to that, a change in location also requires the duck to get accustomed to the new conditions, because of which, laying is significantly reduced.

• **Predators or Pests**: Like we mentioned in earlier chapters, ducks are at the bottom of the food cycle. As a result, they are easily frightened. If your duck has been attached by a predator or even feels threatened by one, you can expect a decline in egg laying. Most often, even pests like rats and rodents will result in stress.

- **The Hen is Broody**: This is a phase that most new duck owners are unaware of. Sometimes, if your duck suddenly stops her prolific egg laying, it is because she is ready for brooding. She is ready to nest the eggs and hatch them. Brooding reduces significantly when collecting of eggs is frequent. Usually, brooding is a habit with younger ducks.

So you see, even if the egg laying comes to a halt, it does not mean that your duck is a poor investment. It only means that you may have to review your husbandry practices or get your duck a good health check up. There are some things that you can do to maximize egg production among your Mallard Ducks. Some steps are extremely simple and will help maintain the cycle of egg production and keep it consistent.

Can I Increase Egg Laying?

There are several steps you can take as the breeder and the owner of your flock to make sure that the egg production is consistent. These simple measures are also very important in ensuring that your eggs are healthy and of great quality.

- **Improve The Quality Of The Feed:** When you purchase the feed from pet stores or the supermarket, you will see that there are several options available. You must make sure that you make no compromises on costs and other factors and only choose recommended duck feed pellets. Make sure that the feed is fresh, has no insects and mold in it and is also compliant with the recommended nutrient levels.

- **Ensure That Your Duck Get The Right Type Of Feed:** The type of food that you choose for your duck must be appropriate for its age. For instance, if you have chicks, make sure you feed them grower pellets instead of regular pellets. Also, maintain the quantity of the feed. On an average, a duck that is ready to lay eggs must be put on a controlled diet. She should be given not more than .35 pounds per day. If your duck becomes overweight, then there are chances that she will develop issues with fertility and egg production. The feed must be removed at the end of every single day while ensuring that it is available to them for the rest of the day.

• **Provide Plenty of Water:** Ducks are waterfowl and definitely require an ample supply of fresh water everyday. Ducks use this water not only for drinking but will also swim in it when they want to. If you are unable to ensure that the water is clean, you will see that egg production is hindered. As I mentioned in the earlier chapters, water is required for ducks to regulate their body temperature. This body temperature is pivotal in the process of laying eggs. If the water is muddy or messy, your ducks will become stressed and depressed to an extent.

• **Ensure Proper Lighting:** Day length is an important concept for ducks that are breeding. Usually, a duck becomes sexually mature only when the length of the day begins to increase. This is between the months of January and June. When the day length begins to reduce, egg production also comes to a halt. If you want your ducks to continue laying eggs despite the available day length, you must make up for the lack of natural light with artificial light. Your Mallard Duck must have at least 17 hours of sunlight every day. This, of course, is greater than the natural light available too. So, in order for your duck to get comfortable with this day length, make sure you add ½ hour of light each day before sunrise and after sunset each week till you reach 17 hours of light

• **Keep Them Calm:** Ducks require a routine. In fact, they are quite fond of the concept of routines. You must give them the same feed each day, provide them with the same type of bedding, the same space to roost in and also the same lighting conditions. If you want your ducks to produce eggs regularly, it is recommended that you even put on the same clothes each time you go out to collect the eggs. Any change in the routine makes the ducks stressed and will reduce their abilities to lay eggs.

• **Do Not Have Too Many Males In The Group:** Usually, the recommended ratio of females to males is 1:5. This ratio must be maintained very strictly if not reduced. However, if you add more males to the group, they will become violent. In many cases, the females get severely injured because of the sexual aggressiveness in male ducks. As a result, the egg laying abilities come down and might even stop in severe cases.

Duck breeding and caring is a matter of great care and responsibility. However, it is quite easy to adapt to if you are able to understand what is best for your ducks. You can also get a lot of assistance from waterfowl experts who will be able to provide you with healthcare and advise to breed healthy ducks.

If you are ever unsure of what to do with your ducks or if you are witnessing recurring health issues, you can check with your local waterfowl expert. He should be able to help you make the right choices for your duck.

The number of eggs that your Mallard Duck lays depends entirely upon the conditions that prevail in your home. You must make sure that the ducks are calm and healthy. If you are sure that the duck does not have anything to worry about during the breeding season, you can be rest assured that you will be able to make great profits due to the numbers of eggs that you will get.

No matter what you do make sure that you prioritize the health and safety of your duck. Keep the environment and other husbandry practices at their best. That way, you will be able to rear healthy ducks that will thrive in almost all conditions. All you need to do is set a foundation that is cordial for your ducks to live and reproduce in. After that, you can enjoy the benefits of having Mallard Ducks on your farm.

If you are bringing home Mallard Ducks for an egg business, you must be patient. It is not something that will flourish overnight. You must be prepared for a few losses initially. Once you learn about handling the eggs properly, you will be able to run your business smoothly.

Chapter 12: Health Concerns for Mallard Ducks

In general, Mallard ducks are very hardy animals. They do not suffer from very many health problems, and are usually resistant to pathogenic viruses, bacteria and fungi.

The best way to keep your Mallard ducks healthy is by providing pristine living conditions and perfect husbandry. This will allow the ducks' immune systems to battle pathogens that they are exposed to.

1. Guidelines to Help Prevent Disease

It is impossible to eliminate the potential for disease transmission. However, by following these three guidelines, you can greatly reduce the risks to your pets, and give them a better chance at living long, healthy lives:

- Minimize the stress on your ducks, so that their immune systems operate at peak efficiency.

- Do not let your ducks socialize. Keep your Mallard ducks away from all other waterfowl.

- Immunize the ducks against as many diseases as possible.

By examining the ways in which different diseases can infect ducks, the reasons for these three guidelines are clear.

In broad terms, some infectious agents are ubiquitous, and only cause problems when they overwhelm an animal's immune system. This is most likely to occur in stressed animals, who do not have access to proper housing, or are fed improper diets. Coccidiosis is one example of this type of pathogen. It infects most ducks, but usually only causes symptoms when a particularly lethal strain is ingested, or when the birds ingest large quantities of the sporulated oocysts (the infectious particles for these parasitic protozoans) (Larry R. McDougald, 2012).

Accordingly, it is important to provide your duck with a clean habitat, feed it the most nutritious diet possible, and ensure that they are protected from inclement weather and temperature extremes, to avoid these types of pathogens, and the illnesses they cause.

Other infectious agents must pass from one host to another, and are not likely to infect ducks that do not come into contact with other ducks. For example, a duck housed singly for the entirety of his life, who does not share water or space with other ducks, is unlikely to develop viral enteritis. However, a duck only needs to sip infected water once to become infected, and ultimately die.

Your flock will undoubtedly exchange germs amongst themselves, so you must effectively quarantine your flock. Try to purchase ducks from the same breeder or retailer, and avoid adding other members to the flock at a later time.

Take care to prevent wild ducks from sharing a pond with your flock. Additionally, be careful when visiting other places with ducks; a frequent way diseases are spread is via dirt particles that cling to people's shoes or clothing. Ensure that visitors have not recently been around other ducks.

Therefore, as explained in the first two guidelines, you should provide your ducks with the very best care possible, to ensure that your ducks' immune system is working as well as it can and that they do not share water, space or the company of other ducks.

Immunization is the process of injecting a dead, weakened or sub-infectious quantity of a virus into a potential host before it gets sick. When this occurs, the ducks' immune systems learn to fight off this virus, while not being at risk of becoming sick. This way, when the ducks eventually encounter the live virus, their immune systems defeat it, keeping them from getting sick.

Some vaccines provide lifetime immunity, while others must be given repeatedly to remain effective. Vaccines exist for duck viral hepatitis, duck viral enteritis and Riemerella anatipestifer infections, and others are under development (Major Viral Diseases of Waterfowl and Their Control, 2011).

By following these three guidelines, you are likely to reduce the chances of illness in your flock significantly.

2. Common Infectious Diseases

Mallard ducks are remarkably resilient animals that are susceptible to relatively few infections and diseases. However, a few are more common than others, meaning that the keeper should pay particular attention to these maladies.

Coccidiosis

Coccidiosis is a protozoal disease that causes ducks to exhibit digestive problems, instability and depression. However, the best clue to the presence of the disease is bubbling from the eyes.

While adults often carry Coccidiosis asymptomatically, it can cause young animals to grow slowly or die. Coccidiosis is treatable with sulfa drugs. However, continuous use of a given drug often leads to the evolution of resistant strains of the pathogen.

Fortunately, a vaccine has been developed to help the birds fight off the infection, and the vaccine is gaining in popularity. Unfortunately, it appears that Mallard ducks are unusually susceptible to the pathogen, which lives in the dirt, mud and water of their natural habitats.

Avian Influenza

Mallard ducks can contract avian influenza, and there is a possibility that they can transmit this illness to humans. Since 1997, the Center for Disease Control and Prevention states that humans have contracted several different strains of the disease.

While wild birds seldom die from the disease, avian influenza is often fatal to captive birds, which often develop more virulent strains of the virus. Waterfowl seem to be especially susceptible to the disease.

A 2001 report documented that the disease caused nervousness and death in a backyard flock of Mallard Ducks and domestic geese (Anser domestica). Upon further examination, the ducks were found to have incurred damage to their nervous systems and pancreases (Mutinelli, 2001).

Riemerella anatipestifer

Riemerella anatipestifer is a bacterial infection that can sicken ducks. Infected ducks are often found on their backs, paddling their legs. Additionally, weight loss, intestinal disturbance and eye bubbling are also potential symptoms.

A vaccine exists for this condition, but antibacterial medications are often helpful for saving ducks with the disease.

Duck Viral Enteritis

Also referred to as "duck plague", this disease can cause ducks to die within a few hours of showing symptoms (Enzo R. Campagnolo, 2001). Your flock could be acting completely normal when you look in on them in the morning and be dead before you start eating lunch. Mallard Ducks appear to be particularly susceptible to this disease (S. Davison, 1993).

Symptoms of the infection include lethargy, anorexia, photophobia (aversion to bright lights), droopiness, nasal discharge and gastrointestinal upset. However, the most common first sign is a massive die off of ducks. This occurs periodically in wild waterfowl populations as well.

There is no treatment for viral enteritis. The only way to prevent the disease is to keep ducks from having contact with other ducks, practice strict hygiene and have all of your ducks vaccinated against the disease. However, the vaccine confers immunity very quickly, and can be used during an outbreak, if administered quickly enough.

Haemoproteus

Haemoproteus is a deadly respiratory infection that can infect Mallard ducks. While Mallard ducks are usually more disease-resistant than Pekin ducks, Pekin ducks exhibit some innate immunity to the infection, while Mallard Ducks can catch the infection from symptomless Pekin ducks (GALT, 1980).

Fowl Cholera

Fowl cholera is a bacterial infection that can infect Mallard ducks. Caused by the bacteria Pasteurella multocida, the disease is highly contagious, and found in waterfowl populations worldwide.

Unfortunately, the symptoms of fowl cholera vary widely. In many cases, one of the first clues is the sudden die off of a large number of birds that were formerly without symptoms. When symptoms are present, they often include intestinal disturbance, rapid breathing, anorexia and depression.

Cholera is usually transmitted via water sources, such as wetlands and ponds. Fowl cholera is a zoonotic, so it is important to recognize the symptoms of the disease and seek treatment for the birds, as it can be transmitted to humans.

Antibiotics are usually prescribed to treat infected birds, but they do not always work. In a 1992 study, fowl cholera was fatal to approximately 50 percent of the birds in the study. The other half of the birds recovered after treatment with antibiotics (Nakamine M, 1992). However, many birds die after treatment stops, which shows that the disease has not been eliminated, but only suppressed.

When a flock is infected with Fowl Cholera, the area must be completely depopulated and cleaned thoroughly to prevent further infection.

Duck Parvovirus

Duck parvovirus is a disease that is especially dangerous to Mallard Ducks. In fact, the disease is sometimes called "Mallard duck disease," or "Mallard duck parvovirus." Primarily a disease of young Mallard ducks, the virus does not cause symptoms in ducks older than five weeks of age.

When young ducks become infected with this deadly pathogen, they only have an approximately 20 percent chance of survival. Hatchlings and young ducklings transmit the virus between themselves, but ducks can also catch the virus from their mother.

Sick ducklings exhibit signs of nervousness, huddle together in a tight cluster and may drag their feet behind themselves. Digestive disturbances may also occur, although the birds do not lose feathers as geese do when infected with the goose parvovirus.

There is no treatment for the pathogen except establishing very strict quarantines and implementing a vaccination program. Day-old chicks can be vaccinated, but the adults must be given boosters regularly to prevent passing the virus to the young, and susceptible, ducklings.

3. Common Traumatic Injuries

Even if you keep your ducks' enclosure impeccably clean, have them vaccinated against common diseases and keep them separate from all other ducks, they can sustain traumatic injuries.

Traumatic injuries are not always as dire as their name implies; they simply occur from an event, rather than a pathogen.

The best way to prevent traumatic injuries from occurring is through vigilantly inspecting their environment for potential hazards. By practicing good husbandry, you can reduce the chances of injury.

Frostbite

While Mallard Ducks often tolerate cold temperatures well, one of the first problems they are likely to experience in very cold temperatures is frostbite. Frostbite is easier to prevent than to treat, so always be sure that your ducks have a shelter that allows them to escape inclement weather. In extreme cases, frostbite can be fatal.

One of the reasons that Mallard ducks are so susceptible to frostbite is that they are warm-climate ducks, who dip their heads frequently in the water. When they pull their heads back out, their delicate facial tissue is wet and exposed to the cold and wind. Their feet sustain damage when the ducks walk on cold, wet ground or snow for extended lengths of time.

If you see that your ducks feet, face or bill have areas that are black, cracked or ulcerated, visit your veterinarian for treatment and fortify their shelter to provide more warmth.

Abraded Feet

Although they look sturdy, the feet of Mallard Ducks are very sensitive to rough surfaces. In severe cases, the ducks can develop serious, systemic infections if the wounds are not cleaned and treated properly.

If you notice wounds or abrasions on your ducks' feet, take them to the veterinarian for treatment. Your veterinarian will likely clean the wound, apply some antibiotics and schedule a follow up exam.

After visiting your veterinarian, it is crucial to fix the problem to prevent further injury. Ensure that all surfaces that the ducks must walk on are smooth and clean to reduce the likelihood of complications.

It also may be necessary to keep your Mallard in an enclosed space while he heals. The bacteria on the ground and in the water may cause the wounds to become infected.

Missing Feathers or Wounds

Ducks lose feathers for a variety of reasons, including infighting, poor nutrition and sickness. Additionally, ducks molt periodically to replace their feathers.

While the first molt you witness may cause you to be concerned, you will soon learn the cycle of molting and what it looks like when the birds go through the process.

However, it is important to distinguish normal molting (and incidental feather loss that happens from normal activity from time to time) from that associated with infighting or disease.

Visit your veterinarian if you cannot determine the cause of the lost feathers. Your veterinarian can perform tests to determine whether or not your duck is suffering from an illness. Missing feathers will usually re-grow with the next molting cycle.

Tangled String and Similar Wounds

Ducks can become entangled in a number of man-made substances, including string, fishing line, rope, netting, plastic or wire. In some circumstances – such as when ducks become tangled while in the water – this can be a deadly problem. Because these types of problems often cause ducks to flail about and struggle frantically to escape, be alert for panicked, struggling ducks. However, if the duck is able to move about relatively normally, they may not exhibit high stress levels, and just try to make the best of the situation.

If you find that your duck is tangled, try to keep it calm while you work to remove the foreign material. Grasp the duck gently but firmly with your arm, while you work the string or wire off with the other hand. It often helps to have another person assist with the procedure.

If your duck is stressed or upset by the activity, it sometimes helps to cover his/her head with a soft, dark cotton bag or towel. Do not wrap it tightly around its head, but let it drape freely. Alternatively, you can take the duck to a dark area, which may also help to calm it down.

After removing all of the material, inspect the duck for wounds. Often, while attempting to free themselves, ducks cause fishing line or similar materials to cut into their skin. If any significant cuts are apparent, consider seeking veterinary attention, as infection is a strong possibility.

If the wounds are minor, use a wound wash or clean water to cleanse the area. Keep the duck in a clean, dry, warm environment for a few days to ensure he/she heals without developing an infection.

Fixing a Broken Wing

The wings of Mallard Ducks form and important part of their defense mechanism and also help them maintain the balance of their bodies when they are running or walking upright. So, a broken wing is a serious issue that must be taken care of immediately.

Of course, you will require the assistance of a waterfowl vet to help take care of the issue completely. However, first aid is necessary when you have a duck with a broken wing to ensure that the condition does not become worse.

There are several reasons why a duck might have a broken wing. If the drakes become aggressive, they are capable of getting injured in fights. Mating among ducks is so aggressive that, many times, the female might be attacked by several males at one time and actually breaks her wings. In addition to this, an attack by a predator may also cause serious injuries to ducks. There are always chances of the wing getting stuck in wires or mesh, leading to injuries like broken bones. Whatever the cause, broken wings can be very painful and must be take care of at the earliest.

A broken wing can cause excruciating pain and can lead to a lot of stress if left unattended. Sometimes, broken wings may also be accompanied by serious cuts and wounds that need to be treated properly to avoid infections. So it is necessary for you to be able to identify a broken wing.

When a wing is broken, it will hang very low. You will notice that it is displaced and is much lower than the other wing.

The first step to treating a broken wing is to gain the confidence of the bird to be able to handle it. Usually when they are injured, birds tend to become more defensive. Especially after an attack, a duck will not really be very easy to hold and take into your care.

First, give the duck some feed and also some water. If he actually begins to eat, it is much easier for you to get a grip on it. However, after a traumatizing injury, your duck is less likely to want to eat. In such cases, the only option you have is to chase the duck to a corner and then catch it. You must be firm in your grip and must gently hold the wings down, taking great care with the broken wing. The best way to calm a duck down is to set her in an isolated spot or even a small cage, which is well lit and warm.

You must approach an injured duck only when you are certain that it has calmed down completely. Failing this, you will find yourself going through the entire process of calming it down again.

Gently examine the bird for wounds and cuts that might be bleeding. These wounds must be washed to remove any impurity that might lead to infection. The wound can be washed with some lukewarm water or even iodine solution. If you have an antiseptic that you have used before, you may apply it.

The next step is to provide a splint or support of the broken wing. You can use sticky gauze or even veterinary tape for this purpose. Hold the wing in the natural position first. It must be held against the body of the bird to make sure that it heals in its natural position. Once the wing is in place, it needs to be bound to the body securely. Take the gauze or the tape around the body of the bird. The objective of the gauze and the tape is to ensure that the wing is immobilized. However, if you tie it too tightly, it might affect the breathing of the bird.

When you wrap the gauze, take it over the broken wing, around the body and under the wing that is functional. This will not restrict the movement of the other wing.

Usually, broken wings take about 4 weeks to heal completely. It is best that you keep the runner in a cage and in isolation until the wing is completely healed. The quality of food must be very good during the healing period. Plenty of water must also be available for the bird to drink. In this period, if the gauze or tape becomes soiled, you may change it.

While you are changing the gauze, if you notice that the duck is able to move the wing comfortably, you can remove the dressing. If not, you can take the gauze off after four weeks. Now your bird is also ready to mingle with the rest of the flock and carry on with his routine.

If your bird has been attacked by a predator, he might require vaccinations or shots to ensure that there is no infection. Even in case of open wounds, it is best recommended that you have it checked by a waterfowl professional.

4. Behavioral Problems

The most common behavior problems that occur in ducks are nipping, pinching and aggression. For most part, ducks are calm and complaisant creatures. Behavior problems usually occur only when the ducks are 6 months of age or older. Aggression is a common problem with drakes who are ready to mate.

It is necessary to curb this type of behavior in the initial years to ensure that it does not persist. If your duck shows any aggressive behavior, a stern and sharp, 'No' should do the trick. However, if the ducks are stubborn, you may also hold the bill and shake it gently, without causing damage to the neck or eyes while repeating a "No". Ducks take time to view their owners as trustworthy companions and not predators.

Stress is also a problem with Mallard Ducks. If you see your duck breathing with an open mouth, flapping his wings often and also refusing to interact with other ducks, there are chances that he is stressed. This may occur due to sudden change in location, extreme weather conditions or even health issues. Your vet will be able to diagnose this problem and provide necessary solutions.

5. Reproductive Diseases

Egg Binding
Egg binding can occur for a number of reasons. The formed egg may be too large to pass through the shell gland or the vagina, the duck may have hypocalcaemia (calcium deficiency) or it may have sustained injury to its vent or vagina.

This often occurs in birds that are of advanced age, extremely young age or are overweight. While the retained egg obstructs the passageway, the duck's body continues producing eggs behind it. Ultimately, this can lead to ruptures or eggs being deposited into the abdominal cavity.

Regardless of the reason it occurs, egg binding is a medical emergency. Ducks that are having difficulty expelling an egg may appear nervous, agitated or depressed. They may walk or pace excessively, as well as exhibit strange body postures.

Unfortunately, this condition is most often noted upon necropsy, as the birds often die before their owner has noticed the symptoms.

If you suspect that a female is egg bound, contact your veterinarian immediately.

Oviduct Prolapse

Sometimes, the oviduct protrudes in the lower region. This condition usually occurs when the duck has difficulty in passing the egg out.

Treatment:
- Provide calcium and phosphorous supplements
- Feed should only include layers pellets
- Keep the duck warm
- Oral medication or injections if the problem persists.

Exposed Penis

Usually, in Mallard Ducks the penis cannot be retracted causing it to drop externally from the body. This may head to infections if it persists. Waterfowl experts associate the upright position of the bird with this problem.

Treatment:
- Keep the environment sanitary and clean
- Provide the bird with lots of drinking water

Meritis

Bacterial infection of the oviduct, leading to inflammation is known as meritis.

Symptoms

- Persistent vaginal discharge
- Loss of appetite
- Lethargy

Treatment

- Antibodies administered orally or through injections

Peritonitis

Peritonitis is usually the result of an ovarian prolapse. When the egg fails to make its way into the oviduct but goes into the abdominal cavity instead, peritonitis occurs. The lining of the abdomen called the peritoneum gets infected.

Symptoms

- Swelling around the abdomen
- Diarrhea
- Sudden Death

Treatment

- Antibiotics have been effective in some cases.

Many breeders put their Mallard Ducks 'to sleep' when they show reproductive problems. Especially if the primary business is egg production, these ducks become a liability. Most breeders resort to this procedure as waterfowl vets can be quite expensive. However, if you are patient, you can help your duck get back to its normal self and produce healthy eggs.

6. Finding a Good Duck Veterinarian

Unfortunately, the veterinarian you take your dog or cat to may not be qualified to treat your Mallard Ducks. Fortunately, finding a veterinarian who specializes in farm animals or birds is not as hard to find as it was years ago.

To find a veterinarian, begin by asking the breeder, retailer or individual from whom you purchased the birds. Often, they will have a relationship with a veterinarian accustomed to caring for waterfowl. If that does not work, you can ask other duck hobbyists in your area.

If none of these strategies allows you to locate a vet, search the internet and local phone listings. If possible, search for reviews of the veterinarian before visiting him or her.

Remember that ducks are not dogs or cats, and a trip to the veterinarian can be an especially stressful event. Therefore, a veterinarian that makes house calls is especially helpful. However, your ducks may require hospitalization or surgery to remedy some illnesses, so it is important the veterinarian has access to a place suitable for such procedures.

Always locate and meet with your veterinarian soon after acquiring your flock. This way, you can become acquainted with the vet if you are not already, and your vet can give your ducks a preliminary physical to ensure they are healthy.

One of the other reasons to visit your veterinarian immediately after acquiring your ducks is to prevent the spread of any diseases they have to their new environment.

For example, if your newly purchased ducks have an illness, and you take them directly from the breeder to your pond, they may spread the disease throughout their enclosure.

Later, when you take them to the veterinarian and have them treated, you must then take them back to their enclosure, where they will become re-infected, thus necessitating further treatment. Additionally, you will be forced to clean the entire enclosure – including the water reservoir – from top to bottom.

Therefore, if at all possible, take the ducks directly from the place you acquire them to the veterinarian's office.

Many duck breeders will determine the gender of the ducks for you, if this is not possible, your veterinarian should be able to determine the gender of the birds for you.

Predatory Attack

While most predatory attacks are likely to end badly for your duck, some ducks do survive such encounters. These episodes have three different problems that must be overcome for the duck to survive.

Initially, the duck must survive the attack. Ducks may be killed from broken necks, damaged organs, profuse bleeding (which can occur internally) or simply from the shock of the attack. Once they have survived this, the duck will need your help to address any significant wounds.

Wash your duck with a veterinary-approved wound wash or, if none is available, clean water. If there are any major lacerations, obviously broken bones or similar symptoms, you must take your duck to the veterinarian immediately. Once these wounds are treated, the duck must survive the last threat from such encounters: infection.

During the healing process, it is important to keep the injured duck in a quiet, calm and clean habitat. Follow your veterinarian's instructions regarding access to swimming water, the administration of medications and any other follow up care.

While attacks are stressful events, with luck and prompt action, you may be able to help your duck survive the encounter.

Poisoning

While not a "traumatic event" by the strictest definition, poisoning should be handled in a similar manner. The symptoms of poisoning vary with the causative agent at work, and are often only determined after ruling out other possible problems.

One frequent cause of poisoning is moldy food. Many molds that grow on wet cereal grains can cause serious illness or death for birds that consume them. Alfatoxins are one of the most important types to prevent. Always ensure that your ducks food stays dry to prevent it from molding. Never feed ducks any food that may contain mold; if there is any doubt in the status of a given food, discard it and replace it with fresh food.

Botulism can occur if your ducks have access to stagnant, warm water, which allows the anaerobic bacteria Clostridium botulinum to thrive. Botulism usually produces a limp paralysis of the neck, wings and legs. Ducks usually lapse into a coma and die within two days of contracting the disease.

Additionally, several chemicals can be very toxic to ducks. Lead and zinc both cause muscle weakness, weight loss and digestive problems. Ducks may ingest lead in the form of old paint chips, lead shot or lead fishermen's weights. Zinc often comes from galvanized metal tubs and fixtures.

Mercury, which is derived from a variety of sources, (including the fish that the ducks eat) also causes weakness. Mercury may stay inside the duck's body (or inside the eggs they produce) for many months after ingestion.

Phosphorus, which is found in a number of rodent poisons, matches and fireworks can be especially deadly. While ducks sometimes exhibit weakness or depression upon ingesting phosphorus, they may also experience very sudden death, in which no symptoms occur.

Even relatively benign chemicals, such as salt, can cause health problems if ingested in large quantities. Salt used to de-ice roads often ends up at the bottom of the watershed – such as your duck's pond. If enough is ingested, ducks may experience convulsions, kidney failure or even death.

Arsenic is another potentially dangerous chemical that your ducks may come into contact with. Used in a variety of poisons, arsenic is also present in some treated lumber. However, if the lumber has dried completely, it will not leach into the environment and harm your ducks. Ducks that eat arsenic show signs of nervousness, and they often die.

Carbon monoxide is an odorless, colorless gas that is often created by heating units. Always be sure that your ducks' shelter is well ventilated if you use a heating device. Carbon monoxide can cause very rapid death in most animals, including ducks.

This chapter discusses some of the most common health issues that duck owners need to deal with. However, if you think that there are other symptoms that you duck might be exhibiting, make sure you take him to a waterfowl expert at the earliest. Never neglect even the slightest abnormality in the health of your Mallard Duck.

The other thing to remember is that you must never provide home remedies and medicines for pets. In case of ducks and poultry you must be additionally cautious as they may have infections that affect our health, too. Make sure you take your duck for routine check ups to keep him in the pink of his health. In case you are negligent you will not only put your health at risk but will also have to shell out tones of money. Remember, taking care of the health of your duck is expensive, as you require the services of specialized waterfowl vets. So the best thing to do is to keep your ducks healthy by providing them with a clean and healthy environment to live in.

Resources

Seek to continually learn more about your Mallard ducks. As with the husbandry of all domestic animals, new techniques and strategies are developed constantly. Never turn down an opportunity to learn more about your new pets, and eagerly seek out those who may know more than you do about these big, beautiful birds.

1. Books

Books can provide information not found on Internet chat rooms and message boards. Books are an especially valuable resource for finding biological information about the species.

Ducks, Geese and Swans: Species Accounts

Edited by Janet Kear

Oxford University Press, 2005

Diseases of Wild Waterfowl

By Gary A. Wobeser

Springer, 1997

Naturalized Birds of the World

By Christopher Lever

A&C Black 2010

Diseases of Poultry

Edited by David E. Swayne

John Wiley & Sons, 2013

Ducks and Geese: Standard Breeds and Management

By George Ellsworth Howard

U.S. Department of Agriculture, 1897

Biology of Breeding Poultry

By Paul M. Hocking

CABI, 2009

Mallard Ducks

By F. Bauer

Papua New Guinea, Department of Primary Industry, 1980

2. Websites

In the information age, learning more about your Mallard ducks is only a few clicks away. Be sure to bookmark these sites for quick access in the future.

Informational Websites

Backyard Chickens

http://www.backyardchickens.com

Though focused on chickens, this website and message board contains plenty of information about Mallard ducks as well.

Poultry Hub

http://www.poultryhub.org/

Maintained by the Poultry Cooperative Research Centre, Poultry Hub provides information regarding all aspects of duck care.

Madiera Birdwatching

http://www.madeirabirds.com/

Madeira Birdwatching provides information about the birds commonly seen on the island, including Mallard ducks.

South Florida Mallard Ducks

http://www.southfloridaMallardducks.com/

This site includes information about wild, feral and captive Mallard ducks.

Mallard Duck Central http://www.Mallardduckcentral.com/

Information about the care and breeding of Mallard ducks.

Backyard Poutry

http://www.backyardpoultrymag.com/

Online magazine featuring news, information and more concerning Mallard ducks and other common poultry.

Ducks Unlimited

http://www.ducks.org/

The world's leading conservation organization dedicated to protecting ducks and their natural habitats.

Cornell Lab of Ornithology

http://www.birds.cornell.edu/

Information about most birds native to North America. This site provides identification photos, sample calls from most species and tips for spotting various species in the wild.

The Poultry Club of Great Britain

http://www.poultryclub.org/

This website provides a variety of helpful resources, as well as information about poultry husbandry and breeding. You can also use this website to find information on breed standards, competitions and meet other poultry enthusiasts.

Xeno-Canto

http://www.xeno-canto.org/

Based in the Netherlands, xeno-canto is a repository for birds sounds, collected from around the world.

Beauty of Birds

http://beautyofbirds.com/

Beauty of Birds has information on Mallard ducks, including information about feral colonies.

The Bird Hotline

http://www.birdhotline.com/

A wealth of information is available on this site. While most is oriented towards parakeets and similar birds, the veterinary resources provided on the website are of value to Mallard keepers.

Breeders

Mallard duck breeders are not only an excellent source for purchasing hatchlings; they can also provide a wealth of information.

The Ugly Duck Farm

http://Mallard.us/

The Ugly Duck Farm produces birds, and provides information on their website for understanding Mallard duck genetics and health problems.

Al's Quackery

http://alsquackery.weebly.com/

Al's Quakery has plentiful information regarding Mallard duck care and color mutations. Additionally, the Quakery offers Mallard ducks for sale when they are available.

J. M. Hatchery

http://www.jmhatchery.com/

J. M. Hatchery breeds and sells a variety of poultry species, including white Mallard ducks.

CaliforniaHatchery.com

http://www.californiahatchery.com/

CaliforniaHatchery.com sells a wide variety of ducks, chickens and other poultry.

Cheap Chicks Poultry Farm

http://cheapchickpoultryfarm.weebly.com/

Cheap Chicks Poultry Farm sells hatchlings and eggs of Mallard ducks and many other poultry breeds.

Metzer Farms

http://www.metzerfarms.com/

Metzer Farms hatches a variety of bird species, and their website provides information about Mallard housing, maintenance and feeding.

University and Governmental Resources

University of Texas at El Paso

https://www.utep.edu/

The University of Texas, El Paso website contains a great deal of duck-oriented information. Of special note are the bird taxonomy resources, which provide information about the classification of ducks.

University of California, Davis

http://animalscience.ucdavis.edu/

UC Davis works extensively with livestock (including poultry), and they work to enhance the lives of captive and companion animals through science.

Duck Research Laboratory

http://www.duckhealth.com/

Maintained by the Cornell University College of Veterinary Medicine, this site provides a wealth of information regarding the husbandry of ducks, including Mallard ducks.

The Poultry Site

http://www.thepoultrysite.com/

Although primarily focused on turkeys and chickens, this Oklahoma State University maintained website contains some information about Mallard ducks.

Animal Diversity Web

http://animaldiversity.ummz.umich.edu/

Maintained by the University of Michigan, the Animal Diversity Web has thousands of pages of information, detailing the lives of various animal species. In addition to reading about Mallard ducks, you can also learn about their predators, prey and competitors here.

Center for Integrated Agricultural Systems

http://www.cias.wisc.edu/

This page, provided and maintained by the University of Wisconsin-Madison, contains a wealth of data concerning all common farm animals, including Mallard ducks.

The Centers for Disease Control and Prevention

http://www.cdc.gov/

Based in Atlanta, Georgia, the CDC provides information on a variety of diseases that may be zoonotic. Additionally, the website provides further resources for coping with outbreaks of salmonella.

Veterinary Resources

Veterinarians.com

http://www.localvets.com/

This site is a search engine that can help you find a local veterinarian to treat your Mallard Ducks.

European Committee of the Association of Avian Veterinarians

http://www.eaavonline.org/

This website includes a veterinarian locator, as well as a long list of links that may be useful for Mallard owners.

All About Birds

www.allaboutbirds.org/guide/mallard/id

A comprehensive website that covers various subjects like life history, care and breeding of different domestic birds.

NC Wildlife

www.ncwildlife.org/portals/0/Learning/documents/Profiles/mallard.pdf

A special compilation of Mallard Duck facts and figures.

AvianBiotech.com

http://www.avianbiotech.com/Index.htm

AvianBiotech.com provides DNA-based lab services to bird owners.

Association of Avian Veterinarians

http://www.aav.org/

In addition to being a good resource for finding a qualified avian veterinarian, this site provides information on veterinary colleges, bird health and basic care.

For The Birds

http://www.forthebirdsdvm.com/

Veterinary and care information for all birds, as well as specific care advice for ducks.

References

- Centers for Disease Control and Prevention . (2014). *http://www.cdc.gov/features/salmonellapoultry/*. Retrieved from CDC.gov: http://www.cdc.gov/features/salmonellapoultry/

- Enzo R. Campagnolo, M. B. (2001). An Outbreak of Duck Viral Enteritis (Duck Plague) in Domestic Mallard Ducks (Cairina moschata domesticus) in Illinois. *Avian Diseases.*

- Fernando GogliAntonia Lanni, C. D.-L. (1993). Effect of cold acclimation on oxidative capacity and respiratory properties of liver and muscle mitochondria in ducklings, Cairina moschata. *Comparative Biochemistry and Physiology Part B: Comparative Biochemistry.*

- GALT, R. J. (1980). MORTALITY IN MALLARD DUCKS (Cairina moschata) CAUSED BY Haemoproteus INFECTION. *Journal of Wildlife Diseases.*

- Hilary S. Stern, D. (2014). *Care and Feeding of Pet Ducks.* Retrieved from For The Birds: http://www.forthebirdsdvm.com/pages/care-and-feeding-of-pet-ducks

- KATARZYNA KLECZEK, E. W.-W. (2007). Effect of body weights of day-old Mallard ducklings on growths . *Arch. Tierz., Dummerstorf.*

- Kear, J. (2005). *Ducks, Geese and Swans: Species accounts (Cairina to Mergus).* Oxford University Press.

- Lack, D. (n.d.). The proportion of yolk in the eggs of waterfowl. *Wildfowl.*

- Larry R. McDougald, P. (2012). *Overview of Coccidiosis in Poultry.* Retrieved from The Merck Veterinary Manual: http://www.merckmanuals.com/vet/poultry/coccidiosis/overview_of_coccidiosis_in_poultry.html

- Mail, D. (2012). That's quite a bill! Prize-winning Mallard drake becomes Britain's most expensive duck after fetching £1,500 at auction . *Daily Mail.*

- *Major Viral Diseases of Waterfowl and Their Control.* (2011). Retrieved from The Poultry Site: http://www.thepoultrysite.com/articles/2051/major-viral-diseases-of-waterfowl-and-their-control

- Mutinelli, I. C. (2001). Mortality in Mallard ducks (Cairina moschata) and domestic geese (Anser anser var. domestica) associated with natural infection with a highly pathogenic avian influenza virus of H7N1 subtype. *Avian Pathology* .

- Nakamine M, O. M. (1992). The first outbreak of fowl cholera in Mallard ducks (Cairina moschata) in Japan. *The Journal of Veterinary Medical Science / the Japanese Society of Veterinary Science.*

- S. Davison, K. A. (1993). Duck Viral Enteritis in Domestic Mallard Ducks in Pennsylvania. *Avian Diseases.*

- SORENSO, K. P. (1999). PHYLOGENY AND BIOGEOGRAPHY OF DABBLING DUCKS (GENUS: ANAS): A COMPARISON OF MOLECULAR AND MORPHOLOGICAL EVIDENCE . *The Auk* .

- Stai, S. M. (2004). Promiscuity and sperm competition in Mallard ducks, Cairina moschata. *University of Miami Library.*

- That's quite a bill! Prize-winning Mallard drake becomes Britain's most expensive duck after fetching £1,500 at auction . (2012). *Daily Mail.*

- Tzschentke, B., & Nichelmann, M. (2000). Influence of age and wind speed on total effective ambient temperature in three poultry species

Published by IMB Publishing 2014

39588694R00089

Made in the USA
Lexington, KY
01 March 2015